□□□□□

www.itchycardiff.co.uk

Globe Quay Globe Road Leeds LS11 5QG
t: 0113 246 0440 f: 0113 246 0550 e: all@itchymedia.co.uk

City Manager	Kelly Halborg
Editors	Simon Gray, Emma Howarth, Bethan Simmonds, Mike Waugh, Andrew Wood
Design	Matt Wood, Chris McNamara
Photography	Dominic Smith
Contributors	Becky Maynard, Jo Rhodes, Alice Boyle, Graeme Dewerson, Shane Kavanagh, James Murphy, David Wilde, Rachel Stanway, Matt Dalby, Sasha Kalokow, Nathalie Grimshare
Acknowledgements	Su Lee, Alex Sutherland

THEY MUST PROMOTE YOU. YOU'VE GOT COMMITMENT.

contents

top fives

itchy cities...

Glasgow
Edinburgh
Leeds
York
Manchester
Liverpool
Sheffield
Nottingham
Birmingham
Cambridge
Cardiff
Oxford
Bristol
London
Brighton
Bath

www.itchycardiff.co.uk

cardiff 2002

Itchy Cardiff 2001 went down a treat, but my oh my, Cardiff's still growing and changing at a rapid rate of knots. We've stripped the city bare and gone back to the roots, reviewing every pub, club, bar, restaurant, gallery and even bowling alleys for crying out loud, to make sure that itchy Cardiff 2002 is bang up to date. We've even added an extra 20 pages, including a Laters section for nocturnal entertainment, local media and completely updated club listings.

itchycardiff.co.uk

What's more, we've finally launched the beast that is itchycardiff.co.uk. Yes, yes, yes – last year, we were just teasing you. But now it's all there in its glory, and you can sign up for a multitude of email and SMS messages – see over for more.

itchy card action

And then there's the itchy card. Last year, we had a set range of offers and venues, but this year, it's tons better. We've already signed up a number of venues to the card, and we'll be adding more, and changing offers throughout the year, details of which you'll find at www.itchycardiff.co.uk All you have to do is turn up to the venue and flash.

Around Cardiff in 1/2 a page

Like last year, we've divided the guide up into sections, but to help your drink-fuelled nights of debauchery, pubs are now split into areas. If you don't know Cardiff, here's a quick round-up.

Roath + Cathays: just outside the town centre, it's where the students hang around. As such expect to find a raw mix of students and locals.

Canton: Again, outside town, this suburb contains a few down-at-heel pubs, but those that we do review are doubtlessly the best of the bunch.

Pontcanna: The salubrious end of Cardiff beyond the Castle by the River Taff. A mixture of fine restaurants, quality drinking holes and upmarket coffee houses.

Centre: Well, obviously it's the hub of Cardiff. As big a mixed bag of venues as you'd find in any city, from the shamelessly grim to the snootily posh.

The Bay/Atlantic Wharf: This area has seen millions poured into its development over recent years. Atlantic Wharf is home to many a swanky bachelor's pad as well as the Leisure Village, whereas the Bay is more offices, in a Canary Wharf-like manner. In the way of entertainment you'll find predominantly restaurants and bars, and a large contingent of meedja crowds.

It's YOUR Red Dragon FM

ALL DAY EVERY DAY

We really are that good to you...

Not only do we write funky little books but we also offer you, the discerning entertainment junkie, some pretty fine stuff on-line.

Point your browser to **itchycardiff.co.uk** and we'll not only keep you entertained with stories and reviews about what's going on in your city, we can also send you regular emails and SMS messages about the stuff you're into. So, we'll keep you informed about where the best happy hours are, when Oakenfold's next in town or where you can find a kebab at 2am. There's also a chance for you to contribute your views and reviews and get free stuff in return (we are too good to you). Have a shoofty. Go on.

Go to www.itchycardiff.co.uk, click on itchyme, and sign up for:

Cheap Drinks / offers • Cheap Eats / offers • House & Garage • Techno & Electronica • Jazz, Soul, Reggae & Funk • Indie • Metal & Alternative | • Hip Hop, R'n'B & Breaks • Drum n' Bass & Jungle • Sixties, Northern Soul & Motown • Seventies, Eighties & Disco • Pop & Rock • | Classical & Opera • World, Folk and Latin • Gay • Comedy • Stage • Art • And all the venues we feature in the book

---

itchy box set

Oh, imagine. **All 16 titles**, an encyclopedia of entertainment across the country, all wrapped up in a glorious multi-coloured special box. Every title below in one mother of a box. Limited edition, naturally, and so exclusive, we don't even know what it looks like ourselves.

Artist's impression. Is this what the box will look like?

If you were to buy these individually, it'd cost you a bargainous £44. But hello, what's this? We're doing the full caboodle **for a mere £35**, including free postage and packing. **Call 0113 246 0440** and order by credit/debit card and we'll whizz one over to you.

bath birmingham brighton bristol cambridge cardiff edinburgh glasgow leeds liverpool london manchester nottingham oxford sheffield york

Two Hours in Cardiff

Right, lets get cracking – you've a lot to see in just two hours. Firstly, no visit to Cardiff is complete without admiring the Millennium Stadium. It'll only take a few minutes, and you'll be glad you did. Move on to St Mary Street and make your way through the arcades that spin off both sides of the street and are full of cool little shops. Thirsty? Then grab a cappuccino at Da Vinci Coffee Shop, Quay Street and enjoy a taste of Italy in Wales (minus the weather). Take a brisk walk past the Castle and towards the Civic Centre where you will find the Museum and Gardens. Then make your way back onto Park Place at the bottom end of Queen Street where, if you've still time, you can window shop in the Capitol Shopping Centre before heading off home. For the less energetic of you who don't want to do so much walking, hitch a ride on one of the Guide Friday bus tours and see the city in under an hour from the comfort of a double decker bus.

Two Days in Cardiff

Day One

This is more like it. For accommodation, check our handy section in the back for anything from a B&B for a mere £25, through to the fully swanky in Cardiff Bay where £65 at the weekend will sort you out with a double room. A cheap option would be to take a wander around the Bay, work up an appetite before sampling the food and drink at Via Fossa or Bar 38. Then get moving onto the Taff Trail – walk for miles or drop down into the Taff Buggy Centre for a spot of quad biking for £16.50/hour. Done?

Shower, change and then get moving straight on to eating, drinking and generally having it. For a meal, take your pick. From the classically sophisticated Cutting Edge to the cheaper but still brilliant Bosphorous, you should be fully ready to move onto the Atlantic Leisure Village and head onto the Evolution club or Rosies bar for a night of mischief.

Day Two

Time to hit the city centre. I know we keep saying it, but no visit to Cardiff is complete without paying a visit to the Millennium Stadium. Go on a stadium tour which costs £5, lasts around an hour and will show you where all of our rugby and football heroes have stood. Next pop around the corner to Cardiff Castle. Stroll around the grounds admiring the peacocks (word of warning – don't get too close) and explore the interior of the castle on one of the tours.

Feeling a bit peckish? Try a superb meal in Life before setting out for a little retail therapy. Spend the afternoon in arcades such as the High Street, Castle, Morgan, Royal Arcades and St David's Arcades – possibly the only way to ensure that the unpredictable Cardiff weather doesn't spoil your visit. To top off your stay in Cardiff go Italian at Da Venddittos or try Thai at the Thai House a set meal for two will set you back £49.45 which should leave you wanting to come back for more.

For the night, take a good look through the bars section and take your pick. Our recommendation for the best club in town? Clwb Ifor Bach. A blinding night for all kinds of music – check itchycardiff.co.uk for more.

■■■ Laters in Cardiff

Late night drinking – Bar M 'til 2am has tapas, comfy leather sofas and live DJs or for something a bit more fancy try The Fontana Wine Bar on Church Street (below Topo Gigio restaurant), which has a late license 'til 2am. At the lower end of town you've got the Metropolis Bar on Charles Street. Fridays and Saturdays see a late license 'til 2am.

Supplies at 4am – Head up City Road off Newport Road and you'll find the 24 hour Spar (029) 2049 0049. Ideally situated in Roath for lashed up students. There's also Tesco Extra open 24 hours on Western Avenue (029) 2042 0700 and Asda 24hr at Cardiff Bay Retail Park (029) 2034 0276.

Late food – Help is at hand by the golden mile of takeaways and chippies on Chip Alley (Caroline Street – located opposite The Square and the corner by Mulligans pub). The best of the fast food haunts is Dorothys Chippy (029) 2064 5813, established in the 1930s, not that you'd care after a few jars.

Tasty late food – If you want a meal minus fries and a polystyrene box then head for The Juboraj Restaurant (Lakeside Road West (029) 2045 5123). Dishing up fine Indian/Bangladeshi cuisine 'til a hardly continental 11pm, but still – it's very handy if you live in Roath or Cathays. Hasapiko on Whitchurch road (029) 2034 2317 opens late most nights serving up your usual Greek fare of mezes and moussaka.

Café society – Bar Europa, 25 Castle Street (029) 2066 7776 has fixed its name on the map of cool cafes with a late drinking license. Art café in the day, and cultured cafe at night. Open 'til late on select nights with writing groups and live music. Another place to slouch and relax in is Floyds on High Street for a street cool vibe and luscious food - open Thu-Sun 7pm-late (029) 2022 2181.

Late night Shopping – Capitol Shopping Centre, located at the lower part of Queen Street, has late night shopping on Thursday 'til 7pm. Queens & St Davids arcade are also open 'til 8pm on Thursday. Other than that take a leisurely drive out of town to McArthur Glen Designer Outlet Village signposted off the M4, open Mon-Fri 'til 8pm.

Late night culture – Films show at midnight on Fri/Sat at the UCI Cinema in the Atlantic Leisure Village 0870 0102030 if you're feeling awake. Closer to the centre is the new UGC complex, where film times extend to midnight for the last showing – call (029) 2066 7667. And OK, not culture, but Riley's pool and snooker halls are open 24hrs on City Road, Roath or Wellington Street in Canton. Take your pick – or cue.

The Welsh have a reputation for drinking and we've uncovered some of the best and worst watering holes in the capital. We've stuffed them into area locations so as not to confuse you after you've had a few jars, but by that stage you won't be able to read anyway. For more details, see the intro pages.

■ ■ ■ Roath & Cathays

■ ■ ■ The Claude
140 Albany Road (029) 2049 3896
Large pub, large screens, pool tables and the resulting hordes of students and skivers. Happy hour runs everyday from 5-7pm with selected pints a mere £1.50, and house doubles £2.10. Cheapskate piss-up heaven. There's always loads going on so check out itchycardiff.co.uk for listings.
Food Served Mon-Sunday 12-3pm

■ ■ ■ The Crwys
Crwys Road (029) 2023 0893
Traditional pub with a sports theme. The walls are splattered with memorabilia, and the rest of the place is scattered with pool tables, dartboards and TV screens. Mondays and Tuesdays offer curry and quiz nights between 7-9pm. Thursdays offer similar echelons of taste and sophistication with rau-

cous karaoke nights – cue underage girls titilating the crowds with 'Like a Virgin', and random old men doing air guitar solos to 'Back in the summer of '69'. Fridays live music is a blessed relief, at least demonstrating some vague semblance of talent.
Food Served 11.30-3pm Mon-Sun, Mon & Tues Curry Night 7-9pm.

■■■ The End
Coburn Street, Cathays (029) 2037 3897
This place rolled straight off the 'how to make a student pub' factory conveyor belt. There are DJs all week, games consoles, pool tables, big screen TVs and drinks promotions galore. If you can't get pissed in here, you've got hollow legs. Quiz night is on Sunday.
Drinks deals, 4 pints £5, Shooters £2.50. No food.

■■■ Ernest Willows
City Road (029) 2048 6235
A typical Wetherspoons pub: Cheap as chips booze (e.g. Grolsch or Hooch 99p all day, everyday) traditional, cheap (if a little ropey) pub food and a spacious layout with no

music. The thing that makes this place stand out is the fountain in the toilets. I'd just sit and drink in there if I had the choice.
Food served 11-10pm Mon-Sat, 12-9.30pm Sunday

■■■ The George
Crwys Road (029) 2043 5901
From the outside this looks like your bog standard old mans boozer, but inside it looks like the 'Changing Rooms' team has just moved out. It's a student pub with plenty to keep you amused – games machines, TVs, pool tables and some tasty totty.
Food Served 12-7pm Mon-Sun

■■■ Pen and Wig
1 Park Grove, Cardiff. (029) 2064 9091
Students rub shoulders with solicitors in this refurbed traditional pub. It's a bit like drinking in a fancy living room with warm lighting, wooden floors and rugs. If you're feeling reflective, escape the masses and snuggle up in a booth to read one of the vast array of books stashed on the shelves. 'Halsburys Statues of England' seems the most popular given the number of editions they've got.
Food Served 12-8pm Mon-Fri, Sat-Sun 12-4pm

■ ■ ■ The Woodville
1-5 Woodville Road, Cathays
(029) 2064 9991
Part of the 'It's a Scream' chain so you can spot it a mile off by the putrid, bright yellow exterior. "I got up at eleven today and really planned to get something done, I mean all I had to do was take my library books back, I just don't know where the day goes..." Bloody students – it's screamingly obvious where the day goes you skiving bludgers – cheap food, cheap drinks, we know where we'd be if we had nothing more important to do than pop to the odd lecture.
Food Served 12-7pm Mon-Fri, 12-4pm Sat, 12-5pm Sunday

■ ■ ■ Canton

■ ■ ■ The Ivor Davies
Cowbridge Road East (029) 2066 7615
The usual offerings from the Wetherspoon's chain. Clinical, boring, no music, cheap drinks and about as much fun as sawing your hand off with a blunt junior hacksaw. OK, that's a bit harsh, but you get the point.
Food Served 11-10pm Mon-Sat, 12-9.30pm Sunday

■ ■ ■ The Maltings
Cowbridge Road East (029) 2064 9081
Built on the site of an old malt house, hence the name. Interested? Neither were we. If you live next door it might be worth stumbling in for a pint, otherwise, leave it be, save your bus fare and don't bother.
Food Served 12-7pm Mon-Fri

top 5 for...
Watching the Footy

1.	Springbok Bar
2.	Sports Cafe
3.	Walkabout
4.	Bar Med
5.	The End

■ ■ ■ Shotz
Cowbridge Road East (029) 2022 7778
The acid bright exterior is supposed to attract the young uns, to entice them into it's inner realm of joy and fun. Don't be fooled. No amount of bargain basement poster paint will stop this place being filled with sad old men drinking the day away in utterly despairing boredom. In fact I'm feeling suicidal just thinking about the place. Ironically enough they have a happy hour between 5-7pm, and the ladies get 2-4-1 cocktails on Tuesday & Sunday nights.
Food Served 12-3pm Mon-Sat

■ ■ ■ Pontcanna

■ ■ ■ Cayo Arms
Cathedral Road (029) 2039 1910
An original drinking den, smack bang in the media metropolis of Pontcanna. With its own brand of brewed ale and food served daily, it's always packed to the rafters. The best pint on offer is the Tomos Watkin Whoosh at £1.70 a pint. A real gem.
Food Served12-8pm Mon-Fri.

■■■ The Beverley Hotel
Cathedral Road (029) 2034 3443

The Beverley seems to cater predominantly for the seasonal influx of American tourists. They come here for two things, the food and to say they've been to one of those cute English pubs – but let's get it right, it's Welsh. Tourists aside, The Beverley is very well respected and serves pretty decent food. My only gripe is the parking. It's a nightmare. Just walk.

Food Served 12-2.30pm, 6-9.30pm Mon-Fri, 12-7.30pm Sunday

■■■ The Poacher's Lodge
Sophia Close (029) 2037 1599

It should have been called The Sportsman's Lodge, since it's mainly the sports management lot from across the car park that wine

and dine in here. The pub itself is beautiful and located near Sophia Gardens.
Food Served 12-3pm, 6-9pm Mon-Sat, 12-4pm Sunday

■■■ Centre

■■■ The Borough
8 St Mary Street (029) 2022 1343

This long, thin pub has a story to tell. It originally opened in 1800 and was the place where the 'bounds' were beaten and the beaters' thirsts quenched. It was then renamed in 1897 to the 'Bodega' putting an end to all this masochism. It remains the tallest building on St Mary Street and was renamed 'The Borough' in 1961. And seeing as we've wasted this whole review with an impromtu history lesson, you'd better get down there and see what it's like for yourself.
Food Served 12-10pm Mon-Thurs, 12-5pm Fri&Sat, 12-6pm Sunday

■■■ Callaghans
Castle Street, (Next to the Posthouse Hotel) (029) 2034 7247

Now whose bright idea was it to put an Irish pub right next to the Millennium Stadium – Wales' most notorious landmark? Ludicrous location aside this is your classic Oirish affair, bikes on walls, faux-aged posters, Danny Boy on the stereo. Contrived, rustic charm mass-manufactured in Milton Keynes. Still, it's open 'til 2am most nights with live bands and hammered locals making their own entertainment. They're trying, really they are. Mon-Sat 11-2am, Sun 12-12am. No Food.

■ ■ ■ The City Arms
10 Quay Street (029) 2022 5258

The City Arms is the ultimate Welsh pub. An old favourite with students, locals, and the odd pop star. Situated directly opposite the Millennium Stadium, the place comes alive when the pub reverberates with songs of jubilation or cries of despair on match days, generally it's the latter unfortunately. Nevermind. Get the pints in.

11-11pm Mon-Weds, Thu 11-1,
Fri & Sat 11-2am
Food Served 12-2.30pm Mon-Sat.

■ ■ ■ The Cottage
25 St Mary Street (029) 2033 7195

A proper, traditional boozer serving up the Welsh brew Brains SA and real cask ales. It's a listed building so you won't be finding any tacky neon lights adorning its facade. And a good job too, this place has got character. The food is homemade and delicious with specials changing daily. Respect going out to the steak and kidney pudding, and get behind us in the queue for Sunday lunch.
Food Served 12-7pm Mon-Sat, Sun 12-4pm

■ ■ ■ Dempseys
Castle Street (029) 2025 2024

Formerly known as 4 Bars Inn, but now fully established as Dempseys Irish pub. It does all that an Irish boozer should do – that is, it serves Guinness amid a friendly, lively atmosphere. There are a couple of big screens and an upstairs theatre/function room. The pub additionally hosts several events during the week such as Twisted By Design (DJ indie night), live bands and the very popular 'Scooters' disco which sees throw backs from the Mod scene get down to a mix of sixties classics with a hint of Northern Soul.

Mon-Thurs 12-11pm, Fri & Sat 12-12
Food Served 12-3pm Mon-Sat

■ ■ ■ O'Neill's
**Trinity Street, Town Centre
(029) 2023 6981**

O'Neill's, O'Grady's, O'Whatever next – this is quite possibly the worst of all the national

Irish chains. About as authentically Irish as Cornetto's are made in Italy. There's a new branch opening in St Mary Street soon, so expect more of the same. Old men, students, and an unsurprising lack of visiting Irish folk.

Mon-Wed 12-11pm, Thurs-Sat 12-12
Food Served 12-5pm Mon-Sun

◼◼◼ Dylans
Park Place (029) 2037 7021

The sign above the door loudly proclaims that they are, 'Licensed to entertain you'. And how pray tell do they intend to do this? It goes something like this. Take fifty desperate women on the wrong side of forty. Combine with an equal measure of balding men, sporting misjudged 'trendy' weekend attire. Shake up with a tack-a-rama of dire chart tunes, and season with the inappropriate molestation of random passers by. Drinks are 80p a throw on Tuesdays – and unless you're teetering dangerously close to the bread line, even these should be approached with caution.

Mon-Sat 11-1am, 12-12.30 Sunday
Food 12-10pm Mon-Sat, Sun 12-6pm

◼◼◼ The Gatekeeper
JD Wetherspoons
9 Westgate Street, Town centre
(029) 2064 6020

The Gatekeeper is a new addition to the pub scene in town, feeding like a leech off the success of the more established Clwb Ifor Bach and City Arms. And not a patch on either. It's a typically soulless Wetherspoon's

affair. The food's cheap, there's a curry club on Thursdays and it's all depressingly average.

Mon-Sat 11-11pm, Sun 12-10.30pm

◼◼◼ Mulligans
51 St Mary Street (029) 2064 4952

If you're an ex-pat or have an affinity with the Emerald Isle then this is the place to be on match days. A truly traditional Irish boozer that doesn't need any gimmicks or tin signs to generate a sense of authenticity. The clientele are older, showing the kids how to have a good time. Join them for a pint of the black stuff.

Food Served 11-7pm seven days

■ ■ ■ Glassworks

4 Wharton Street (029) 2022 2114

The Cucumber has been renamed and revamped as the Glassworks. It's amazing what a lick of paint, cleaned carpets and a name change can do, but you ain't fooling me. It's still the same old average boozer trying too hard to be a bar. To its credit the food is cheap, as are the regular cask ales, such as Abbots, IPA and Old Speckled Hen, and the monthly £6.95 wine offers. Don't all rush at once.

Food Served 12-8pm Mon-Sat

■ ■ ■ Old Monk

St Mary Street (029) 2039 5933

A big, brash, towny cattle market. Still interested? Well, I guess someone has to be. The Old Monk is new in town and proving fairly popular with its inviting sofas and packed out dancefloor. Drinks offers run all day from Monday to Wednesday, and weekend DJs send crowds of flailing freaks to the floor. Most bemusingly there's a sign to the disabled toilets pointing downstairs – handy.

Mon& Tues 11-11pm, Wed 11-12, Thurs 12-1am, Fri &Sat 12-3am

Food Served 12-9pm Mon-Sunday

top 5 for...
Playing Pool
1. Sports Café
2. The Corporation – Shotz
3. The End
4. Springbok Bar
5. Riley's

■ ■ ■ The Owain

John St. (Next to RSVP) (029) 2022 1980

After countless name changes this boozer has finally settled on The Owain, an ode to the Welsh fundamentalist Owain Glyndwr. A decent place for some pub grub or a real cask ale. Check out the specials boards for offers on food and drinks.

12-11pm Mon-Fri, 12-12 midnight Fri & Sat

Food Served 12-9pm Mon-Thurs, 12-8pm Fri & Sat, 12-9pm Sunday

■ ■ ■ Prince of Wales

82 St Mary Street (029) 2064 4449

Start that night you can't even hope to remember here. If there's one place on a weekend pub crawl worth retaining memories from then it would probably be this. It's themed around the original theatre decor, with Royal boxes intact. Other than this it's fairly run-of-the-mill, large and carpeted with cheap drink deals. Check out the 'Stairway to Heaven' – a local legend, not for the short-skirted or self-conscious.

Food 11-10pm Mon-Sat, 12-9.30pm Sun

YOU'RE IN AN INTERVIEW

■ ■ ■ The Rummer Tavern
Duke Street (029) 2064 9871

At last, an unpretentious chain pub. The place has got a true sense of character and a proper pub atmosphere. Nothing special, nothing fancy, just a decent pint, a few cheap drinks offers and a traditional pub menu – cracking stuff.
Food Served 12-7pm Mon-Sat

■ ■ ■ The Toad
The Old Library, The Hayes
(029) 2066 6566

Thank God they dropped the 'Slurping' prefix, as the concept of knobbly amphibians with badly evolved table manners was enough to put anyone off their rum and coke. What remains is The Toad, a no frills hangout offering Wednesday night karaoke, tequila slammers and cheesey student nights. Weekends are messy and packed with punters enjoying a night devoid of the need to dress with style, dance with finesse or engage anyone in intelligent conversation.
Mon-Tue 12-12am Wed-Fri 12-1am, Sat 12-2am, Sun 12-10.30pm
Food Served 12-6pm Mon-Sat

■ ■ ■ Walkabout
65-74 St Mary Street (029) 2072 7930

Tacky, Aussie theme pub with zero subtlety and ridiculously cheap drinks. This is the kind of place that tends to refuse groups of blokes, but likes letting in couples and pissed-up girls. This we'd imagine is partly to provide footage for the video screens dis-

Page 7
www.itchycardiff.co.uk

playing the dancefloor action. Whoever is in charge of the camera, shamelessly zooms in on the easiest available crotch/cleavage shot and these get progressively more risqué as the night wears on. It's a bit like late night Home & Away – so watch it girls. Other than that, it's always packed, with big screens, DJs on the weekend and a cover band on Thursdays – anyone for a bit of Clouded House? Food is served up daily with a bizarre menu offering big brekkies, sarnies and snacks to the Carnivore Corner. How about trying a bit of Skippy (Kangaroo Steak) for £5.90?
Food Served 12-10pm Mon-Fri, 12-7pm Sat, 12-10pm Sunday

DON'T GET INTIMIDATED BY THEIR EYE CONTACT

top 5 for...
Outdoor Drinking

1. The Wharf
2. Callaghans
3. The Poachers Lodge
4. The Eli Jenkins
5. The Beverley

■■■ The Bay

■■■ The Eli Jenkins
7 Bute Terrace (029) 2044 0921

One of only a few pubs in the Bay and pop-ular with locals and tourists alike. The food is great value with plenty to choose from (mains start at £3.75), house doubles are fixed at a line 'em up £2, and the atmosphere is relaxed and traditional. The pub overlooks the breathtaking Oval Basin and Bay, making it an ideal place to watch the world go by. If that's not enough to keep you entertained there are big screen TVs showing sport. And if that still doesn't entertain you, you'd prob-ably be better off ogling the hordes at Walkabout, or you need to go on holiday to Disneyland, and get a wide-screen TV for when you get back. And a Playstation II.
Food Served 12-9pm, Mon-Sat, Sun12-7

■■■ The Packet
95 Bute Street (029) 2046 5513

Situated near the developing Mermaid Quay area of the Bay, The Packet has a warm, invit-

ing feel and plenty of tourist appeal. There's a big emphasis on food which is surprisingly cheap for the quality. The weekly specials boards show dishes of the day but you can't beat the curry of the day served with chips and rice for £3.50. Cultured, sophisticated and terribly authentic.
Food Served 12-2.30pm Mon-Sat

■■■ Sports Café
**Graving Docks, Cardiff Bay
(029) 2045 9000**

A massive, sports-themed drinking venue split into several sections – a bar area, restaurant, amusement area and dancefloor. Fitting for a big all day session, but equally good as somewhere to take the nippers out for a bite to eat. The focus is on letting your hair down and putting the mundane dreari-ness of nine to five behind you, and if your

 "OI, WHAT ARE YOU LOT STARING AT!?"

girlfriend is boring you to tears you can take out your pent up aggression in the indoor basketball area. Worship at the altar of the great God of sporting activity – it's big screens and rugby chants all the way. Rock up to watch Wales get battered again in the footy or rugby. And drown your sorrows 'til midnight (2am at weekends).

Mon-Thurs 12-12am, Fri & Sat 12-2am, Sun 12-10.30pm

Food Served 12-12am Mon-Sat, 12-10pm Sunday

■ ■ The Wharf
121 Schooner Way, Cardiff Bay
(029) 2040 5092

Beautiful pub by the harbour and squaring up to a metropolis of snazzy apartments and penthouse suites. Location aside this place offers the best live entertainment for miles around. There are weekly live bands and stand-up comedians. It's an unpretentious chillout zone with good food and a lively feel. They won't tell you off for singing at high volume, and if you fancy escaping outside for a chat, there's seating aplenty with swanky harbour views.

12-12am Mon-Wed, 12-1am Thurs-Sat, 12-10.30pm Sunday

Food served 12-10pm Mon-Sat, 12-9pm Sunday

■ ■ Floyds
St Mary's Street (029) 2022 2181

A shameful omission from our bar section we know – but fortunately we noticed just in time. Floyd's is a small bar, above its namesake clothes shop, catering for Cardiff's twenty-something trendies. It's laid back, swanky and making an effort on the exclusive side of things – well hidden from the local riff-raff. The food's good, especially the desserts – so rock up for a refined cocktail and a slice of cake in your best outfit. It's all glamour, though it has to be said the excessive Robbie Williams on the sound system kind of detracts from the cool factor. And even though we've put it incongrously in our pub section we're saving ourselves a year's worth of abuse for missing it out.

Thu-Sat 7-11 (we think).

Meal for two: £22 (Satay chicken)

Gemma, 22, Barrister

Best place for relaxing after work?
Probably Incognito I guess
Posh. And then on to a club maybe?
Liquid's always a safe bet
Salubrious. How about a restaurant?
Pearl of the Orient. I take it that's not an offer.
What do you love about this city?
The bay development – truly magnificent
And hate?
Tricky. It'd have to be trying to catch a taxi on Saturday nights

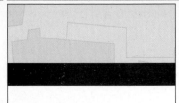

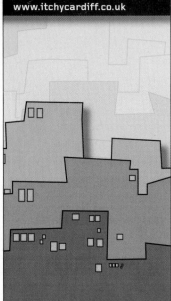

www.itchycardiff.co.uk

The bar scene in Cardiff has exploded since our last guide, so here's the best of the bunch. The cost of a meal for two is worked out using the price of two main courses and a bottle of house wine.

■■■ Amigos
11 Windsor Place (029) 2023 8228

Like a surreal Mexican car-boot sale, Amigos is full of rustic bric-a-brac masquerading as carefully contrived décor. Add to this a no fuss menu, a piss-up atmosphere and you'll be shouting 'arriba, arriba' and downing terrifying shots before you can say 'by jove these Mexicans know how to throw a party'. There's a revamp on the cards – bringing a pool table and slouchy sofas to the skiving student masses. The restaurant downstairs will remain as it is, with a happy hour everyday from 4-7pm and 9-10pm Mon-Thur. Shooters drop to £2 on Friday and Saturdays 9-11pm, there's also a big screen for sports and a heated beer garden.

Mon-Thur 11-11pm, Fri/Sat 11-1am, Sun 11-7
Meal For Two £18.85 (Mixed grill)

■■■ Bar 38
Stuart Square, Mermaid Quay, Cardiff Bay (029) 2049 4375

This is your average, contemporary chain bar. Identikit minimalism, posturing crowds and just enough sophistication to make you swop your usual lager and lime for something a bit more refined. There's an upstairs balcony, a varied menu and night time DJs spinning Hi-Fi delux sounds to an up-for-it crowd of revellers.

Mon-Thur 11-11pm, Fri/Sat 10-1am, Sun 10-10.30pm
Meal For Two £25.95 (Shared meal option)

EEL THE

RE SENCE

PATRICIA GRANT,
FASHION DESIGNER

A MELLOW MIX OF SPIRIT AND SOUL
THAT FLAVOURS WHATEVER IT TOUCHES.

MORGAN
SPICED

top 5 for...
Cheap Drinks

1. Sams Bar
2. Springbok Bar
3. Bar Med
4. Cuba
5. Is It?

■ ■ ■ Bar Essential
33 Windsor Place (029) 2038 3762

In London or Bristol this would just be your average poncey bar, somewhere to knock back a swift one on your way somewhere else. But stick it in Cardiff and people reckon it's all a bit swanky – it's a decent enough place serving up vodka cranberrys to the Cardiff professional set and the kind of students that spend all their money on DKNY underwear. Check out the Rev James Cask Ale, Brains and Murphy's at the bar along with monthly guest ales – it's not all girly cocktails and bottled foreign lager.
Mon-Sat 12-11pm
Meal For Two £20.15 (Thai green curry)

■ ■ ■ Bar Europa
25 Castle Street (029) 2066 7776

Bar Europa operates on a pretext of arty culture, though it's more of a cross between an Ikea café and a French Youth Hostel. Join the baffled foreign exchange students with ruck sacks on their fronts and get down to a surreal sing-a-long. If your idea of high culture is MTV mixed in with a bit of random poetry you'll be happy comparing sandals with your new Euro-pals here.
Sun 11-4pm, Mon 11-6pm, Tue-Sat 11-11pm

■ ■ ■ Bar M
31 Westgate Street (029) 2034 3330

The M certainly doesn't stand for music policy. During the day, we're talking Take That and Geri Halliwell on repeat, but don't let that put you off. At night the place is buzzing, with the Cardiff cool-set fighting for space and falling out over the last comfy sofa. The club downstairs booms and shakes to salsa rhythms on Thursday nights, classes are from 8.30-10.30pm, and there's plenty of time to practice your fancy footwork with a disco 'til 2am. Fri and Sat sees the DJs move in and the place reverberate to a charty house beat. Tapas is served upstairs 'til 2am amid more neutral sounds. Chill out with a game of Blackjack.
Mon-Sat 11-2am
Meal for two £25.05 (Chicken wings, nachos, olives & cheese)

■ ■ ■ Barfly
Kingsway, Town Centre (029) 2025 5533

Barfly at London's Monarch has launched many a struggling, guitar wielding wannabe

◼ ◼ ◼ Bar Med
Pearl House, The Friary, Town Centre
(029) 2022 5063
Bar Med is always rammed, quite inexplicably so at times. It's your usual blistering yellow walls, boisterous punters and bottle deals combo. But with a sinister Jeckyll and Hyde twist. By day it's an innocent, pleasant escape from work/shopping hell with good value lunch specials. Come the evening it metamorphoses into a beast of party choons, Bacardi Breezers and happy hours – watch out for the last minute rush to the bar between 11.30-12.30 – worse than wearing a Swansea shirt on the Cardiff terraces. Oh and cattle market is an understatement – if you can't pull here it's time to join a dating agency.
Sun 12-10.30pm, Mon-Wed 11-11pm, Thur 11-12 midnight, Fri/Sat 11-2am
Meal for two £24.65 (Hot grilled tuna)

into the music industry stratosphere, and Cardiff's offering is set for more of the same. A dingy, dark, live venue with a real buzz about it. Cardiff has been crying out for somewhere like this – a welcome alternative to chain bar overkill. Check out bands on the brink of record deals – there are three a night strutting their stuff on stage.
See itchycardiff.co.uk for listings.
Mon-Wed 7:30-11 Thurs 7:30-1 Fri & Sat 7:30-2
No food served.

◼ ◼ ◼ Bar Ice
Churchill Way (029) 2023 7177
Bar Ice, like its counterpart Reds across the road, attracts town revellers and university students, who descend upon its chrome bar like magpies hypnotised by the reflecting metal and pounding music from the club downstairs. They've dropped the lame attempts at a music policy and opted for cheese and chart all the way. Not for teetotallers – you've got to be pissed to have a good time in here. Great for a no holds barred bender and a guaranteed snog.
Mon 10am-11pm, Tue 10-12 Wed-Sat 10-2am, Sun 12-4pm.
Meal for two £23 (Malaysian spicy noodles)

◼ ◼ Brava
71 Pontcanna Street (029) 2037 1929
Arty café set in the middle of the media

A MELLOW MIX OF SPIRIT AND SOUL.
THAT FLAVOURS WHATEVER IT TOUCHES.

metropolis. Brava's combination of sumptuous food and drink, art exhibitions and flash

interior design appeals to even the fussiest of air-kissers. As such you'll find it buzzing most nights, with well-dressed pretty types comparing filofaxes over a chilled glass of Sauvignon Blanc (or perhaps us with our skanky jotter pads). It's worth checking out – an itchy favourite.

Mon-Sat 9-6pm, Sun 10-4pm
Meal for two £16.85 (Eggs benedict)

■■ Cafe Calcio
145 Crwys Road, Roath (029) 2039 7575
Home of the Fat Bastard, quite possibly the best, lard ridden breakfast in Cardiff (£5.50) only feasibly finished by its namesake. This is the ideal place to cure the hangover from hell and amiably swear at waiting staff, which is all too necessary after a night when you've been blown out, kicked out of a club and run over by a taxi. I should know.

Mon 10-3pm, Tue-Fri 9-5pm, (Friday only)7.30pm-12am, Sat/Sun 10-7pm
Meal For Two £11 (Fat bastard brekkie)

■■ Cafe Jazz
St Mary St (029) 2038 7026
Jazz aficionado heaven. If jazz is your thing then this is the place for you. From your traditional plucking and strumming on Tuesday with the Jazz Preservation Society to Latin/jazz shenanigans on Wednesday nights. Thursdays see the big names in jazz descend for the evening, whereas Mondays Jazz Attic opens the stage to wannabe Duke Ellington's and Miles Davis's. Bring your instrument and show 'em what you're made of. There's bar food from 12-3pm during the day and a restaurant 'til late.

Mon-Sat 11-1am (Food orders 'til 10.30pm)
Meal For Two £21.50 (2 Course special lunch menu)

■■ Cameo Club
Pontcanna Road
(029) 2022 0466
If your name's not down you're not getting in. Cameo is an exclusive, underground haunt frequented by Pontcanna's media darlings. But take heart – downstairs the membership policy has been relaxed and now any random pleb can drink in the lower bar. Here you'll find a chilled feel and sophisticated, art dèco style. Check out the famous Cameo breakfast, (£3.95), served 'til a very civilised 5pm. Upstairs is members only in the evening and if you want to join them you'd better be prepared for a wait; there's a hundred on the list before you.

Mon-Sun 9am-2am
Meal For Two £20.45
(Cajun spicy stir fry)

◼◼ Café Mina
43 Crwys Road (029) 2023 5212

Filled from the minute the clock strikes five with posh students who'd rather sell their kidneys to medical science than suffer the indignity of tinned spaghetti hoops. If they were in London they'd arrive on those mincing little metal scooters, but fortunately here they don't. The idea here is to 'chill' you 'funky young things'. So 'get with the program', and don't choke on that onion ring. No really, don't.

Mon-Fri 5pm-11pm, Sat/Sun 11-11pm
Meal For Two £22.85 (Chili con carne)

◼◼ Cibo Italian Café Bar
83 Pontcanna Street (029) 2023 2226

Sit and watch the world go by Mediterranean style in this recently refurbed café bar. If you're hard enough to brave the Welsh weather, then hang out in the back garden and enjoy a killer cappuccino. The restaurant's excellent and always rammed, so booking ahead is advisable.

Mon-Sat 10-10pm (food 'til 9pm)
Meal for two £21.50 (Roasted veg pannini)

◼◼ Cuba
The Friary, Town Centre (029) 2039 7967

One night at Cuba will do more for your Latino spirit than the company of ten, naked, gyrating Ricky Martins in a penthouse suite at the Hilton. The live music induces a spontaneous, hip-swinging and sexually-charged atmosphere, while Tuesdays £1 tequila shots are a disaster waiting to happen. Thursdays offer live funk bands and Bacardi Rigo at £1.50 a bottle. Weekend DJs (resident Andy Loveless) spin funky beats 'til 2am and happy hour runs from Mon-Sat, 5pm-9pm (2-4-1 cocktails, £5 pitchers of beer). Get in there.

Mon-Thur 11-1am, Fri / Sat 11-2am
Meal For Two £16.60 (Chicken & chips)

◼◼ Fontana Wine Bar
Church Street (029) 2034 5903

Classy Italian wine bar below the popular Topo Gigio restaurant. You gotta be wadded to drink in here – they have to pay for the decorating somehow, I suppose. More sofas than a DFS showroom, though unfortunately they don't offer interest free credit.

Mon-Sat 5pm-2am, Sun 5-12am
No food

top 5 for...
Late Drinking

1. isit?
2. Bar M
3. Metropolis
4. Life
5. Springbok

■ ■ ■ Ha-Ha Bar and Canteen
The Friary (029) 2039 7997

Finally a Cardiff café bar has managed to strike the balance between young and funky without being insultingly pretentious. Ha Ha has got it spot on, with a laid back music policy and impressive food – join the queues for the weekend brunches. The menu consists of 'things to nibble and munch', 'canteen food' and 'proper food', all well-presented, simple, fresh and served in sizeable portions. And once you've got addicted to their sauces, you'll be pleased to

know they're all on sale. Things get more lively at weekends and on match days they play host to Cardiff's more cultured sports fans with big screen TVs and maximum enthusiasm. Highly recommended.
Mon-Fri 11-11pm, Sat 10-11pm Sun 10-10.30pm
Meal For two £24.50 (Chargrilled lime and coriander chicken salad)

■ ■ ■ Henry's
8-16 Park Chambers, Park Place
(029) 2022 4672

Part of a nationwide chain, Cardiff's Henry's is pretty much the same as he is everywhere. Décor wise it's dark wood and a peculiar shade of lighting that makes everyone look like they've been tangoed. That aside the place dishes up reasonable food at prices you wouldn't argue with (although your gran might). Down Champagne cocktails for £4.75 or stay true to your roots with a common-as-muck £2.50 shooter.
Mon-Sat 9-11pm, Sun 12-10.30pm
Meal for two £24 (Battered hake on bubble and squeak)

■ ■ ■ Incognito
29 Park Place (029) 2041 2190

Classy bar and restaurant with a sophisticated atmosphere – all a bit disconcerting when you're clad circa 1993 with a Kwik Save carrier at your side. Still, it suits the solicitor suits and students with trust funds crowd just fine. Happy hour from 5pm 'til 8pm Mon-Sun with a pleasant, easy-going vibe, rather than a rack 'em up and get 'em lashed

panic kind of feel. This is somewhere to relax and impress during the day, and get down to the blaring DJs at the weekends.
Mon-Wed 8am-11pm, Thur-Fri 8am-2am, Sat 12-2am, Sun 12-10.30pm
Meal For Two £21.00 (Chicken & veg skewers)

■ ■ isit?
Wharton Street, Town Centre
(029) 2041 3600

'Is it what?' – you could take an instant dislike to this place on account of its name alone, and if they ever get implicated in some kind of politician-related sexuality scandal the Mirror would have a field day with puns. Shit name aside the place has style. It's less identikit than the rest of the kids on the block, offering high backed chairs and plenty of booths to misbehave in. Packed with office bores, talking spreadsheets during the day, and by night the same crowds loosen their ties and let their hair down for an evening of drinks promotions and cheap chat up lines. Happy hour is daily between 5-7pm with house wine at £5.
Mon-Wed 11-11, Thur 11-1am, Fri/Sat 11-2am, Sun 12-10.30pm
Meal For Two £19.00 (Risotto and cajun Tuna Steak)

■ ■ ■ Las Iguanas
8-8a Mill lane (029) 2022 6373

Yet another in the long list of Latin American bars which most of us have now grown tired of. However this is one of the better ones. By day a colourful, yet tasteful place to enjoy some decent South American tucker. By night a tack-fest of party tunes. A new menu has just been introduced offering regional dishes from Brazil and Puerto Rico – two courses will set you back an entirely reasonable seven quid. Cocktail happy hour is between 5-7.30pm with two-for-one offers and one hell of a crowd to fight through at the bar.

Meal For Two £21.50 (3 Course meal)

■ ■ Life
St Mary Street (029) 2066 7800

Life has definitely made its mark on Cardiff's city centre – a large queue-shaped one on a Saturday night. Once you've made it past the door you'll find a mix of swank sophistication and lots of focal features. Check out the flat wall TVs, art displays and cool design. The appeal basically lies in the incongrous blend of laid-back atmosphere and dancefloor tack. Steps routines sit comfortably alongside polite conversation and Semillion Blanc . Life is fun. There are plenty of eventful theme nights – check out the Latin classes on Wednesdays. It's also known for its cheap daytime menu, two main courses £5.50 and 2-4-1 offers during happy hour daily.

Mon-Thu 4pm-11am, Fri & Sat 12-1am, Sun 7pm-12am

Meal For Two £20.45 (Oriental duck salad)

■ ■ Metropolis Bar
Charles Street, Town Centre (029) 2034 4300

Metropolis sounds like it should be the sleaziest club in town, conjuring up images of seventeen year old slappers with perms and men of a certain age sporting comedy bow ties. However, it is anything but – this is a classy bar and restaurant, oozing style, with more modern art on its walls than Saatchi's living room. Even the bar snacks are cultured. Chill out, sink a few spritzers and sing along to the John Lennon lyrics plastered on the walls. Check it out.

Mon-Thurs 12-11pm Fri & Sat 12- 2am.
Food: Mon-Fri 11-3pm, 6pm-11pm (all Sat)

Meal For Two £34.10 (Red mullet)

■ ■ Oz Bar
112 St. Mary Street, Town centre (029) 2066 8008

About as Australian as Catatonia but don't let that put you off. The atmosphere in this place is as active as your arthritis-ridden granny and there's more culture in an ashtray. Let that put you off.

Mon & Tues. 11-11 Wed-Sat 11-1am, Sun 12-12am

Meal For Two £11.99 (Meal deal)

artificial intelligence ••

Available from Tesco, Waitrose and other leading wine and spirit retailers. Also available from Bar 38, Casa, Henry's, J D Wetherspoon, The Rat and Parrot, Via Fosse, RSVP and other independent bars and restaurants.

For more information call 020 8943 9526

www.seborabsinth.com

■ ■ Reds Café Bar

**Churchill Way, Town centre
(029) 2064 1111**

A sports bar you say? I'd never have guessed. Red's is a little bit of of the U S of A transported into the heart of Wales. The place is plastered in NFL posters and general sporting regalia. However it seems the only kind of activity the clientele here are in training for is the drinking olympics. They stick to their schedule with an impressive display of pride and commitment. A few warm up exercises early in the afternoon, a quick sprint (shooters at 7pm), followed by some weight lifting (raise Guinness to mouth, and down – repeat), a spot of synchronised swigging and possibly the high jump when you get home. Mon11-11pm, Tues-Thur 11-1am, Fri 11-2am, Sat 11-2am, Sun 12-10.30pm
Meal for Two £18.45 (Chicken korma)

■ ■ RSVP

St John Street (029) 2022 1980

RSVP? I'd rather leave ASAP. Formerly known as the 'Owain' – a mecca of madness and drinking on match days. Now it's filled with neon lights, unnecessary glitz and artwork depicting bygone rugby victories. As such it still attracts a crowd of revellers and rugby lads on match days and weekends. They must be drawn to the pumping handbag house and moody doormen.
Sun 12-10.30pm, Mon-Wed 11-11pm, Thur-Sat 11-1am
Meal For Two £18.90 (Chicken curry)

■ ■ Sam's Bar

63 St Mary Street (029) 2034 5189

The corner stone of Mill Lane and the café quarter is Sam's Bar – miss it and you definitely need to go for that overdue eye test.

top 5 for...
Pulling (Fussy)

1. Ha Ha Bar
2. Metropolis
3. Fontana Wine Bar
4. Life
5. Is It?

Outside there's table service for drinks on rare sunny days. Inside it's bright with a chrome finish. Décor aside, this is one of the best live music venues in town with a line up of hot local bands and the odd well-known artist. Weekends nod in the direction of commercial chart and retro tack with bargain drinks prices.

Mon-Fri 11am-2am, Sat 11am-4am, Sun 12pm-1am (licensed 'til 12.30am, food 'til 6pm)

Meal For Two £16 (Spaghetti bolognese)

▮ ▮ Slug & Lettuce
2-3 Working Street (029) 2034 1616

Average and non-descript. If the Slug & Lettuce was a bloke in your office, he'd be Dave in accounts. By his desk he'd have in pride of place, a photo of him holding aloft a freshly caught and slightly larger than average sardine, his greatest life achievement to date. He'd listen to M People and think that the Lighthouse Family were good but a bit risqué, and his dream woman would be Lorraine Kelly. Got the picture? There's also a big screen for sports, but it's hidden away at the furthest end of the bar so on match days the place swells at one end – like viewing an image through a sieve. No slugs, a bit of lettuce and a lot of Daves.

Mon-Sat 11-11pm, Sun 12-10.30pm

Meal For Two £21 (Caesar salad)

▮ ▮ ▮ The Springbok Bar
Mary Anne Street, Town centre
(029) 2039 5899

New addition to the bar scene but this time with a South African theme. Massively popular for it's extensive array of TV screens – twenty-four in total, two pool tables and a sixty foot bar serving indecently cheap drinks. Oh, and before I forget, there's a preposterously over-sized rugby ball – and before you even think about it, look but don't touch, or they'll 'ave you. Chill out in the zebra skin booths and slurp at a cocktail or two. Food is served daily with a lunch time two meals for £5.95 deal (11-6pm).

Mon-Wed 11-11, Thur 11-12,
Fri & Sat 11-1am

Meal For Two £15.50 (Chicken stinger – That's its name, the portions are huge)

top 5 for...
Pulling (Unfussy)

1. RSVP
2. Bar Emporium
3. Paparazzi
4. Bar Ice
5. Reds

A MELLOW MIX OF SPIRIT AND SOUL.
THAT FLAVOURS WHATEVER IT TOUCHES.

■ ■ ■ The Square
78-80 St Mary Street, Town centre
(029) 2022 1170

A night out at the Square is a bit like being forced to take part in the Rocky Horror Picture Show – sinister, disturbing, and not much fun. There are two floors, a massive Rubik's Cube of TVs and a big central bar. It's an alright place to go if you hate the people you're with – you'll lose them in seconds (if they don't just leave in disgust). There's cheap drinks offers, 'buy one cocktail and get the next for 25p' and vodka Red Bull for £2.90, if you're still reading.

Mon-Fri 5pm-11pm, Sat 11-11pm,
Closed Sunday

■ ■ ■ Toucan Bar
95 St Mary Street, Town Centre
(029) 2037 2212

The Toucan has landed in its new city centre home (see club section for a more extensive review). The bar is as popular as the club and open during the day with an ethnic, individual, arty feel. Check out the global cuisine, excellent Toucan brekkie (£4.50) and evening tapas. There's a line-up of funky DJs and live jazz on Sundays – not to be missed.

Tue-Sat 9am-2am, Sun 9am-10.30pm

■ ■ ■ Via Fossa
Mermaid Quay, Cardiff Bay
(029) 2045 0947

The medieval feel to this place makes you want to order meat by the plateful and slam your pewter down on the table, demanding that a court jester entertain you. The reality is that you'll wait an age to get served and no doubt get a slap in the chops if you request a buxom wench to do the same.

Mon-Sat 11-11pm, Sun 12-10.30pm
Meal For Two £22.35 (Red Thai chicken curry)

■ ■ ■ Yates's Wine lodge
8 Westgate Street, Town centre
(029) 2034 0957

Yates's – and why would we even bother to expand on that. Well, frankly we wouldn't. You know the score, you know what you're in for, on your own heads be it.

Mon-Wed 10-11, Thu 10-1am Fri/Sat 10-2am
Meal For Two £17.50 (Brie and bacon tart)

restaurantsrestaurantsrestaurantsrestaurants **restaurants** ■ ■

restaurants

www.itchycardiff.co.uk

With more restaurants than you can shake a chopstick at, half the problem in Cardiff is choosing where to eat. Let itchy guide you through the minefield of culinary delights in the city – to illustrate the price we've taken a main dish (stated in the brackets), doubled the price and added the price of a bottle of house wine to estimate the price for a meal for two. Oh, and we've yet to find a decent African eatery, so if you open one up, give us a shout.

■ ■ American/Pacific

■ ■ Bourbon Street
Cowbridge Road East, Canton
(029) 2025 7177

A very Canton take on the Deep South. However, what this family-run restaurant lacks in authenticity it more than makes up for in atmosphere. Get stuck in to the char-grilled, barbecued, sweet and spicy menu and forget everything your mother ever taught you about eating in polite company. The homemade, potent, hangover-inducing cocktails are also well worth checking out.
Mon-Sat 11-11, Sun opening times vary.
Meal for two £15.90 (Bourbon Street Platter)

■ ■ Diner 77
77 Pontcanna Street, Pontcanna
(029) 2034 4628

Meedja centralis; join Cardiff's AbFab set, Marilyn Monroe and James Dean for top-notch, classic American diner fare. We're talking big portions all round, calorie-laden desserts and fries with everything. Being in the posh part of Pontcanna, they get packed with long suffering parents enduring their kid's birthday party meal out. Cue loud

whinging and fist fights over who's got the best Pokèmon collection. Thankfully there's a fully licensed bar – get slowly slaughtered and drown out their demands for more ice-cream.

6-11pm Mon-Sat, 6-10pm Sun
Meal for two £22.85 (77 Mega Burger 12oz)

■ ■ ■ The Hawaiian Pacifico
17 City Road, Roath (029) 2049 3337
This Hawaiian restaurant initially seems rather run of the mill; maybe a touch too flowery, possibly revealing the faintest hint of tack and teetering precariously on the loud side of well behaved. But nothing, repeat nothing, can prepare you for the scenes of hula-ing debauchery in store as the Pina Coladas kick in. Seeing is believing; hammered hen nights, office workers on a bender and chanting students, downing lurid shots, showing off their disco moves and limboing like they've never seen a low positioned pole before.

Mon-Sat 7-11
Meal for two £26.85 (Huli Huli Chicken)

■ ■ ■ TGI Fridays
7 City Link, Newport Road (029) 2046 0123
Take one family-sized helping of screaming brats, mix in some party hats, a screeching rendition of Happy Birthday and some mountainous American-style grub, and voila, dinner is served at TGI Fridays. Catering for the family night out, it isn't everyone's idea of fun, and the over-poweringly hi-five friendly service can slip into the GBH-inducing side of nauseating, but it's still as popular as ever. The Ultimate Cocktails are the biggest in town, and mouth-watering desserts such as Mocha Mud Pie prove a significant draw to the Cardiff masses.

Sun-Thu 12-10.30, Fri/Sat 12-11.30.
Lunch/early evening menu 12-7.30
Meal for two £32.20 (Blackened Cajun Chicken)

■ ■ Chinese

■ ■ ■ BJ's
Barry John's Oriental Kingdom
Westgate Street (029) 2022 7771
An incongruous combination of oriental cuisine and rugby memorabilia – ex-Welsh rugby star Barry John runs the joint. It sounds ludicrous but somehow it works, probably because old BJ leaves the cooking to chef, Tony Lee, imported from Kuala Lumpar. Tony knows his stuff, with food a mix of influences spanning Malaysia, Thailand, Canton, Szechuan and Peking. All you can stuff in your mouth £9.95 buffet lunches pull in the crowds and they offer a range of set-menus and banquets. Handily situated opposite the

Millennium Stadium, it's generally full of ex-pats chewing over old times, or businessmen chewing over today's Times.
12-3, 6-11.15 Mon-Sat, 12-4 Sun
Meal for two £49.85 (Millennium Meal)

■■ Fortune House
43-45 Salisbury Road, Cathays
(029) 2064 1311
The kind of place that gets over-looked by most local folk, on account of it being dumped unceremoniously in the heart of the student district. This, for half of our readers, makes it a cracking place to stagger into on a Saturday night, after falling out of the pub next door. The other half should check it out during the week when the students are too busy swopping internet porn and pouring water on their supanoodles to make it out of the house. Very good, truly authentic food.
Mon-Sat 12-2, 5.30-11.30, closed Sun
Meal for two £32.95 (set veggie dinner for 2)

■■ Happy Gathering
233 Cowbridge Road East, Canton
(029) 2039 7531
The food here is utterly fantastic, and its popularity with the local Chinese community plays testament to this. They recently closed down for a few months to have a refurb, then re-opened with not so much as a stencilled dado rail to their credit. When questioned about this mysterious lack of Changing Rooms type activity it transpired that their idea of a refurb is to do up the kitchen. Still, if it makes 'em happy it's good enough for us.
Mon-Thu 12-11, Fri/Sat 12-11.45,
Sun 12-10.30
Meal for two £39.80 (Set Meal for 2)

■■ Noble House
St David's House, 9 Wood Street
(029) 2038 8430
Famous for its Sunday dinner – but not roast beef and Yorkshire puds, rather the £9.90 'all you can eat' menu. That aside, we're talking prices to make you weep like a child with a militantly efficient clinical feel. The place is like a motorway – good at doing the job, but mind-bendingly boring.
Lunch 1pm one sitting, Mon-Sun 6-11.30
Meal for two £34 (Szechuan Set Menu)

■■ Pearl of the Orient
Mermaid Quay, Cardiff Bay
(029) 2049 8080
It's a newly established Oriental restaurant in the ever-developing bay, and a plush affair at that. Modern, swanky features such as the fish tank bar, water doors and novel window displays of scrumptious food (you can't eat them – leave off) set this apart from any of your preconceptions of a standard Chinese restaurant. Traditionally clad staff serve up set meals for £14 per head with surprising courtesy and charm. Unusual, we know. Takeaway coming soon.
Mon-Sun 12-12
Meal for two £62 (Oriental Feast & Shoaxin Wine)

■ ■ ■ Riverside Cantonese
44 Tudor Street, Riverside (029) 2037 2163

This place has got a reputation. A bit like that girl at school who charged the boys 10p a go to look up her skirt, but somewhat more prestigious. They first opened in 1977 and they've been building a reputation for the finest Cantonese fare in Cardiff ever since. If it's good enough for Egon Ronay...

Décor is strictly traditional, with water features and an open-plan dining area. You can also indulge in the sinister pleasure of selecting the fish or lobster of your choice for slaughter. Nice. The bar area is cracking too – San Miguel on draught and plenty of space for reclining pre - or post-meal .

12pm-12am Mon-Sat, 12pm-10pm Sun
Meal for two £40.70 (Set Menu & HW)

■ ■ ■ European

■ ■ ■ Cutting Edge
Discovery House, Scott Harbour, Cardiff Bay (029) 2047 0780

A bit like calling yourself Hot Stuff Henry or wearing a t-shirt with 'God I'm gorgeous' emblazoned across the front. You're clearly setting yourself up for a fall, or some kind of public ridicule. Cutting Edge has somehow managed to avoid both despite the show off moniker. The place is classy (with a home counties accent) attracting Cardiff's more discerning drinkers to the bar and power lunching MPs to the bistro. The big, showy windows ensure the plebs outside can see you and your sophisticated choice of dinner venue. Smooth down those stray eyebrow hairs, laugh uproariously at your date's dazzling company and muse over how far you've come since those rowdy piss-ups at Pizza Hut. Flash

food and fancy décor done to perfection.
Mon-Fri 8am-11pm, Sat 6pm-11pm
Meal for two £47.40 (Roast Rack of Lamb with Mustard and Herb Crust)

■ ■ ■ Dealto
**Mermaid Quay, Cardiff Bay
(029) 2049 1882**

Can't be arsed to cook? Don't want to get too dressed up but fancy something a bit more nourishing than the mouldy baked-bean pizza festering in the back of your fridge? Dealto's dish up carefree ad-hoc meals in what resembles more of a cafe than a restaurant, albeit a Mediterranean one. Decidedly chilled out, with a down-to-earth menu of salads, pizza and pasta, it's cheap, cheerful and popular.

12-2.30, 6-9.30 Mon-Thu, 12-3, 6-10 Fri & Sat, 12-3, 6-9.30 Sun
Meal for two £25.55 (Luinguine con Pollo alla Mediterranea)

■■■ Gilby's

Old Port Road, Culverhouse Cross
(029) 2067 0800

Warm, inviting, relaxing and bloody expensive. Teetering precariously between, 'this is swanky and the food is gorgeous' to 'this is wanky and the price is outrageous' sits Gilby's. For romantic meals and creating impressions of casual wealth, you can't do much better. Recently awarded the coveted Michelin 'Red M' prize for its culinary masterpieces, Gilby's reputation goes from strength to strength. Try the Early Bird Menu of 3 courses for £13.95 available 'til 7.15 Tue-Fri and 'til 6.30 Sat. Dress smartly, put on your best table manners and be impressed.

Tue-Sun 12-2.30, 5.45-10pm, closed Sun eve
Meal for two £36.85 (Chargrilled Yellow
Fin Tuna)

■■■ Hullaballoos

92 St Mary Street (029) 2022 6811

The dictionary defines its name as, 'a loud confused noise, especially a protest or commotion'. Come about 8pm, the place does resemble a G8 summit, albeit a more peaceful one. Food is a healthy mix of traditional British dishes with a twist of Europe thrown in for good measure. Relatively quiet and sedate until the hordes arrive.

Tue-Sat 12-3, 6-9
Meal for two £40.50 (3-Course Set Dinner)

■■■ Metropolis

60 Charles Street (029) 2034 4300

Fast becoming the number one choice for Cardiff's sophisticated, twenty something, pre-club crowd. It's swanky and sophisticated with a cocktail bar feel. Downstairs you'll find sofas, booth style seating and art adorn-

edge

Wine Bar & Bistro ....

Discovery House
Scott Harbour
Cardiff Bay
t: 029 20470780
f: 029 20440876

ing the walls. Upstairs is classy restaurant territory with an interesting mix of modern dishes, anything from mullet or monkfish to duck and Welsh lamb. And there's a home grown range of flavoured vodkas to work your way through in between courses.

Mon-Sat 12-3, 6-11
Meal for two £34.10 (Red Mullet)

■ ■ ■ French

■ ■ ■ La Brasserie

60 St Mary Street (029) 2037 2164

Low lighting and wooden ceilings add to the rabbit warren, authentic feel of this restaurant. It feels like you could have just stepped in off a sundrenched Brittany sideroad. There's an open plan kitchen so you can see how they're treating your crustacea before they get to your plate. It's all very fresh and quite delicious – check out the huge chillers displaying their wares to get an idea of what's in store.

Mon-Sat 12-3, 7-12.30am
Meal for two £37.35 (Fillet Steak)

■ ■ ■ Le Cassoulet

5 Romilly Crescent, Canton
(029) 2022 1905

You come, you eat, you fall in love. No, it really is that good – an exquisite, quaint French restaurant, run by a lovely couple from Toulouse. To add to the authenticity, and that intriguing sense of pot luck ambiguity about what you've ordered, the waiters speak French, and to ensure complete confusion, the chefs are Argentinean. But no matter. The service is impeccable, wines spectacular and the rustic feel insurpassable. Be impressed.

Tue-Sat 12-2, 7-10
Meal for two £41.50 (Le Cassoulet)

■ ■ ■ Le Gallois

8 Romilly Crescent, Canton
(029) 2034 1264

L'argent monsieur, and plenty of it. Plush as you like, and held in high esteem by the multitude of certificates and awards plastered around the place. So well-to-do, that it gives you the unsettling feeling that you're really not well-heeled, well-connected or well-

dressed enough to be here at all. Get out oik, Nicky Wire eats here don't you know?
Tue-Sat 12-2, 6.30-10
Meal for Two £61.50 (Set 2 course meal)

top 5 for...
Fine Food
1. Cutting Edge
2. Benedictos
3. Thai House
4. Le Cassoulet
5. Tomlins

■ ■ Greek

■ ■ Aegean Taverna
117 Woodville Road, Roath
(029) 2034 5114
Working on the principle that mystery sells, they've put up massive one-way mirrors on the outside of this restaurant, to try and intrigue passers by into stepping inside. And the ones who don't find themselves inside what they first assumed to be a secluded sex shop hidden behind the façade of Greek salad and moussaka, don't seem to be too disappointed. Food is classic Greek, with meze options and plenty of fish and vegetarian options. Smashing (both the plates, and the restaurant), and although it really shouldn't be encouraged, you can carry on the Greek theme back in the bedroom.
Mon-Sat 7pm-11
Meal for two £28.25 (Souvlaki Platter)

■ ■ Hasapiko
72 Whitchurch Road, Heath
(029) 2034 2317
Fancy reliving those holiday memories? Well rock up here for an overdose of Ouzo, meze's, dips, moussaka and plate smashing 'til the early hours. All that's missing are the swarms of mosquitoes on a piss-up by proxy blood-sucking mission and an overly enthusiastic moustached man called Andreas, intent on pulling your girlfriend. Well, you can't have it all, hey?
Mon-Sat 6.30-11.30 (last order)
Meal for two £30.50 (Moussaka)

■ ■ Indian/Bangladeshi

■ ■ Balti-Wallah
Cowbridge Road East, Canton
(029) 2023 1227
This place, although licensed, offers the option of BYO, just don't try turning up with a crate of lager under your arm – you're only allowed to bring champagne or wine. Not that we're sure there's enough car stereos in South Wales for Balti-Wallah's dodgy punters to afford such extravagant liquor. Regardless of this the food ain't half bad,

- Juboraj one of Wales most renowned award winning restaurant group
- A mix of modern and traditional Bangladeshi / Indian cuisine presented in unique ways
- Enhanced style, intimate atmosphere which brings back the discerning customer making it a high spot to see and be seen in

Juboraj Lakeside Restaurant, Lake Road West, Cardiff Tel: 029 20 455 123 - closed Mond
The Juboraj Restaurant, Heol-y-Deri, Rhiwbina, Cardiff Tel 029 20 628 894 - closed Sund
The Juboraj Restaurant, 10 Mill Lane, Cardiff Tel: 029 20 377 668 - closed Sunday

Open six days a week
www.juboraj.co.uk

house specialities are Punjabi and Kashmiri dishes, and the atmosphere's pretty relaxed. Besides, everybody knows that drinking champagne with curry is only for uncouth idiots or Frenchmen.

Sun-Sat 12-2, 5.30pm-12am (1am Fri/Sat)
Meal for two £11.90 (Fresh Cream Pasanda)

■ ■ Café Naz
Mermaid Quay, Cardiff Bay
(029) 2049 6555

Your concept of a decent curry largely depends on whether you were born closer to Bradford or Basingstoke. This place is of the disarmingly clinical, tidy up after yourself and behave nicely persuasion. So leave your pissed persona at the door, and appreciate the speciality cuisines on offer – Bangladeshi, Banarasi and South Indian offerings along with plenty of seafood and vegetarian dishes. All delicious enough to make up for the lack of pissed-up rugby players.

Sun-Thu 11-10, 11 'til late Fri/Sat
Meal for two £23.40 (Lamb Dabba Xacutti)

■ ■ Juboraj
Juboraj Lakeside
Lake Road West, Roath (029) 2045 5123

One of the most celebrated names in terms of Asian cuisine in Cardiff, specialising in Bangladeshi and Asian sub-continent. The lakeside restaurant is one of many Juboraj restaurants dotted about the city set in the idyllic back drop of Roath Park Lake making it the perfect setting for an intimate date or family meal. Incredibly, they've managed to shun shouts of 'Vindaloo!' for an altogether more relaxed, classy and intimate affair.

Tue-Sun 12-2.30, 6-11
Meal for two £24.85 (Chicken Tikka Massala)

■ ■ King Balti
131 Albany Road, Roath (029) 2048 2890

King Balti isn't one for regal pretensions; in fact his crown's probably gathering dust in an old shoe box while he concentrates on building up his culinary empire. Not content with serving up a range of Balti dishes, there's now Japanese, Thai, Chinese and Malaysian fodder on the menu too. They claim to be the first Balti house in Wales, but considering that was in '87, a full 12 years after they came to Birmingham, you've got to wonder if they couldn't have moved just a tad faster. Still, they're here now. Don't let the ominous stuffed rooster in the cage outside put you off this place. It's well worth a look.

5.30-11.30 (12 Fri/Sat)
Meal for two £29.95 (Chefs Subzi Special)

Becky, 18, Student

Student eh? So for cheap drinks?
Springbok Bar every time
Thought so. How about best club?
V2K most nights is lively as..
OK, so for a meal. Bearing in mind you're on a student grant. Las Iguanas
You're well-dressed though. Best shop?
Top Shop
More like it. Best thing about Cardiff?
It's hectic and bustling
And the worst?
No beaches dude (she really said this)

PIERO'S

- 100 seater function suite

- Party menu available

- DJ's Fri & Sat 9-2 am

- Local art exhibits

- Takeaway serv

- Lunchti speci

- Downstai 60 seat ristoran

P

PIZZERIA
RISTORANTE

185 COWBRIDGE ROAD EAST, CANTON, CARDIFF, CF11 9
TEL NO: 029 20 227060

■ ■ Italian

Cardiff has got Italian restaurants galore, so forgive us for missing out the delights of Pizza Hut. There's far too many places to list here, so outside of our mentions below, highlights of different areas include Giovanni's on the Hayes, Topo Gigo and Positano on Church Street, all near the Millennium Stadium, Mamma's on Churchill Way, Valentino's on Windsor Place, La Lupas in Canton and Mamma Mias in Roath.

■ ■ Cibo Italian Café Bar
83 Pontcanna Street (029) 2023 2226
Emerging from a recent make-over, this small Italian still rules the roost in luvvie-land Pontcanna. There's a cracking back garden for long lazy summers and nowhere near enough tables inside to accommodate the hordes of families and couples that flock here for the excellent food, wine and cosy cafe feel – book first or be disappointed.
Mon-Sat 10-10pm (food 'til 9pm)
Meal for two £21.50 (Roasted Veg Pannini)

■ ■ Da Venditto's
7-8 Park Place (029) 2023 0781
This swanky Italian is only two minutes walk from the theatre, and as such makes a popular pre/post pit stop for a classy taste of Italy. The place oozes sophistication (no bloody

pizza), but at a price, naturally. Conversation with staff is limited to a few simple words – 'your bill, thank you'. How very Italian.
Mon-Sat 12-2.30, 6.30-10.45
Meal for two £51.50 (Sea Bass)

■ ■ La Strada
Wesley Lane (off Charles Street)
(029) 2022 2242

Cosy and intimate with first class service. Tucked away, just off Charles Street, we rate this place for those special tête-a-têtes. Make sure they're worth it though as it's quite pricey, unless you go for lunch when it's only £7 for two courses (she'll never know), or the Wednesday night dinner special offers of three courses for a tenner. Inside, it's a fairy-lit wooden affair with candlelit tables. Traditional, but reassuringly cosy.
Meal for two £40.85 (Duck in Cherry Sauce)

■ ■ Pieros
185 Cowbridge Road East, Canton
(029) 20227060
Pieros, with its clean, modern décor takes the faux grapevines and suspended salami out of your rustic, local Italian joint. There's a

party feel with DJs on Friday and Saturday nights and the food is consistently good.
Meal for two £30 (Antipasti/pizza/bottle of wine)

■ ■ ■ Trattori Pulcinella
9 Park Lane, Town Centre (029) 2034 0397
Just about as hard to find as it is to pronounce, but worth the effort nonetheless. Trattori is the opposite of Pieros, with Chianti bottles galore dangling from the ceiling. Split into three levels, with intimate table seating this is a good place for hot dates and piss up birthday parties alike. There's your usual pizza, pasta offerings – nothing outrageously exciting, but all well-prepared in the open-plan kitchen and damned tasty.
Filetto Vesuvio £35.90 + wine

■ ■ ■ Japanese

■ ■ ■ Izakaya
**Mermaid Quay, Cardiff Bay
(029) 2049 2939**
The best Japanese in Cardiff. Well actually the only Japanese in Cardiff. But that said, it's all beautifully done in an entirely traditional

way. Small tables, lanterns, a matted area that allows you to eat with your shoes off and two rooms for larger groups. The food is excellent, bar the minging Green Tea ice-cream and the menu extensive. In fact the only problem with this place is the refined sense of quiet sophistication – pressure to behave always spells disaster and Cerys Matthews was once thrown out for being rowdy – so try and stay sober. The bar serves

up Kirin, naturally, and Fosters (well, there's always one fussy tosser). Set lunch is served daily for £8.
Mon-Sat 12-2.30, 6-11pm, Sun 1pm-10pm
Meal For two £45 (Set meal-6 Dishes)

■ ■ ■ Lebanese/Moroccan

■ ■ ■ Casablanca
3 Mill Lane (029) 2064 1441
A café bar and restaurant offering authentic Moroccan and Lebanese cuisine amid traditional Arabic surroundings. The menu is packed with choice for meat-lovers and veggies alike and fortunately there's an English description underneath each unpronounce

able name so there'll be no unexpected surprises. A house favourite has to be the 1001 Arabian Night where you can take a peak into the sheikh's tent and be entertained by a belly dancer. You should try it – a little bit of the Middle East in the centre of Cardiff minus the bombs and street violence (although Saturday nights here offer enough violence of their own). Décor comes complete with large swords on the walls to deter bill-evaders.

12-12 Mon-Sat
Meal for two £29.85 (Kubba bil Saynayeh)

■ ■ Mexican

■ ■ El Paso
120 City Road, Roath (029) 2046 2054

El Paso, el shittio, el crapo, el hellholio, el she-dio. Wade through the clutter of ponchos, sombreros and tequila and you might just find a seat. Though you'll wonder why you bothered with the sub-standard food and service. This place has a lunar atmosphere, so at least there's no surprises.

5.30-11.30pm seven days.
Meal for Two £25.30 (Fajitas)

■ ■ Las Iguanas
8 Mill Lane (029) 2022 6373

Where would we be without the humble chain restaurant? Well, we'd have no formu-laic fun, no manufactured in Swansea 'authentic' Mexican interiors, and no identik-it home fries to get our teeth round on a Friday night. That said, this example's not too bad, with more of a focus on the entertain-ment than the food. Burritos, fajitas and a small army of happy hours and cheap eats offers thrown together with enthusiasm. It's pretty good as a bar and the atmosphere from the club downstairs filters upstairs to keep the youthful diners buzzing. Watch out on itchycardiff.co.uk for groovy special offers.

Sun-Thu 12-11, Fri/Sat 12-1am
Meal for two £ 26.50 (Xinxim – Brazilian Lime Chicken with Shrimp & Peanuts)

■ ■ Portuguese

■ ■ Lanterns
41 Whitchurch Road (029) 2061 9988

Lanterns, Lanterns, Lanterns – come and have a go if you think you're hard enough. One of just three Portuguese eateries around town, and if the bunch of miserable monkeys who serve you are anything to go by, good job too. Don't let the rustic lanterns and subdued outdoor lighting fool you; inside it's an entirely under-whelming experience both in food and service.

6-30-12 Mon-Sat
Meal for two £30.50 (Steak Portuguese)

! 🗋 ✏ From	Subject
✉ itchycity.co.uk	Restaurant recommendations via e-mail

■ ■ ■ Madeira Restaurant
**2 Guildford Crescent (off Churchill Way)
(029) 2066 7705**

The self-proclaimed, one and only, authentic Portuguese restaurant in Cardiff. It thankfully lives up to its Chesney Hawkes-style claim, packing out every night with a crowd happy to come back for more. They attract carnivores with plenty of hefty meat dishes, and more clean living types with the originally titled 'Healthy Food' section on the menu. Ten out of ten for literal naming. Still, don't let it put you off, it's such a small thing.

12-2.30, 6-11 Mon-Sat. Closed Sun
Meal for two £26.85 (Chicken Piri Piri)

■ ■ Spanish

■ ■ Benedicto's
4 Windsor Place (029) 2037 1130

If Benedicto raised a family the kids would be seen and not heard, dressed in head-to-toe M & S and would run away with a strange tribe of graffiti artist spiritual types to live in a squat in Brixton at the first opportunity. It's oppressively serious in here. Tuck into your Mediterranean and Spanish food, mind your Ps and Qs while you're at it, and look – you're using the wrong bloody fork. No, outside in, you ignoramus. Have you been brought up or dragged out? And so it is with Benedicto's, priced out of the reach of the

LOOK AT HIM, POMPOUS IDIOT.

...ess well to do diner anyway, except at lunchtimes, when two courses for £13.50 makes it plausible.

Mon-Sat 12-3, 6 til late
Meal for two £45.50 (Fillet of Salmon)

■ ■ Thai

■ ■ Thai Empire
6 St David's House, Wood Street
(029) 2066 8838

Situated incongruously between a Chinese, an Indian and the bus station. Fancy it most certainly isn't, but they've thoughtfully done their best to give the illusion of class by hiking the prices sky high. How considerate. They ban under-7s at the request of customers, but you can tell your kids they're not missing out on much. Snobbish and over-rated.

Mon-Sat 12-2, 6.30-11.15
Meal for two £46.90 (Set Meal for 2)

■ ■ Thai House
3 Guildford Crescent (off Churchill Way)
(029) 2038 7404

This is more like it. The first Thai restaurant established outside of London, extended recently due to its huge popularity. They do things properly here from the authentically dressed staff to the dishes presented like works of art. Even the timber flooring is the result of careful restoration from the floor of the old Philharmonic Theatre. This, along with the two original stone fireplaces, creates a calm, contemporary ambience. There's a light and airy bar area, and a menu offering exotic and unusual spicy dishes. It's pricey but well worth the money – the staff are friendly, the atmosphere's buzzing, and blow me if this place isn't good.

12-2.30, 6.30-11.15 Mon-Sat
Meal for two £49.45 (Set Meal for two)

■ ■ Turkish

■ ■ Bosphorus
Mermaid Quay, Cardiff Bay
(029) 2048 7477

Newly opened in Cardiff Bay, this is a highly popular retreat for those looking to re-enact those sun-drenched holiday memories.

TOO BUSY DIGESTING HIS FOUR HOURS
LUNCH TO LISTEN TO YOU

Situated on a jetty overlooking the harbour, its modern appearance is enhanced by the old artefacts from the 18th century docking days. If you're not acquainted with Turkish cuisine it's primarily orientated towards succulent slabs of meat jazzed up with herbs and marinades and exotic fresh fish dishes. The daily lunchtime menu is a mere £7.95 and the à la carte isn't priced much more. A dining experience with a difference.

12-12 Mon-Sun
Meal for two £30.40 (Apricot Glazed Chicken)

■ ■ ■ Vegetarian/Vegan

■ ■ ■ Beaz Neez
Wyndham Arcade (029) 2033 1478

Specialises in vegetarian and vegan cuisine so expect to leave with a spring in your step and a fully rejuvenated karma. There are plenty of hearty options and tasty desserts to put paid to the myth that healthy eating is all about nibbling on bird seed and green leaves.

10-4 Mon-Thu, 10-8 Fri, Sat
Falafels/Samosas £3.50

top 5...
Eats To Impress

1.	Cutting Edge
2.	Bosphorus
3.	Gilbys
4.	Juboraj
5.	Le Gallois

■ ■ ■ The Greenhouse
38 Woodville Road, Cathays
(029) 2023 5731

Less Greenhouse, more primary school classroom, with dinky wooden chairs and squashed-up tables. Still, at least you're paying for the food in here rather than Feng Shui consultancy fees and specially carved toothpicks. Real home cooking and an ever-changing, delicious menu, enough to shatter any preconceptions about vegetarian food.

Tue-Sat 12-3, 7-10
Meal for two £33.50 (2-Course Set Menu)

■ ■ ■ Tomlins
46 Plassey Street, Penarth (029) 2070 6644

The majority of restaurants in Cardiff have about as much interest in vegetarian cuisine as Europe does in British Beef. And rugby players aren't renowned for their love of lentils. But there's still plenty of veggies, and thank God for this restaurant – dedicated to bringing out the chic in chick pea, which makes a refreshing change. The garish yellow exterior belies hidden delights within.

WELL, DIGEST THIS!

it's small, intimate and airy, perfect for a chilled out, meat-free evening out.
Tue-Sat 7-12.30, 11.30-2.30pm Fri/Sat, alternative Sun12-2.30
Meal for two £28.65 (Aduki Bean & Mushroom Packages with Mushroom Broth & Fennel)

■ ■ Welsh

■ ■ The Armless Dragon
97 Wyeverne Road, Cathays
(029) 2038 2357
Like eating in an extended living room, albeit an exceedingly posh one. Taking Welsh food to another level, the Dragon, armless or not, manages to rustle up some extremely tempting dishes. These come highly recommended by us (should you care what we think) and a million and one restaurant guides. Welsh classics all served with a quirky twist.
Tue-Fri 12-2, Mon-Thu 7-9.30, Fri/Sat 7-10
Meal for two £34.90 (Brecon Lamb with Carrot & Red Lentil Puree & Rosemary)

■ ■ ■ Blas Ar Gymru
(Taste of Wales)
48 Crwys Road, Roath (029) 2038 2132
The best Welsh restaurant in the capital by far, attracting swarms of tourists wanting a taste of Wales before heading home. It's all very homely, a bit like eating at your favourite aunties but with a higher class of culinary expertise, not dissing your auntie or anything. Savour the aroma, and while you're at it, make sure you sample the traditional specials – you can't beat a bowl of cawl on a cold winters day or a rack of fine Welsh lamb. Welsh food at its finest, and as such, a firm favourite at itchy.
Meal for two £37.85 (Salt Duck)

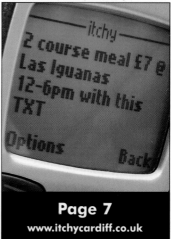

Page 7
www.itchycardiff.co.uk

 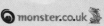

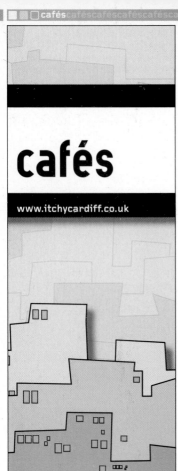

cafés
www.itchycardiff.co.uk

Coffee war has been declared in Cardiff, with chains and independents lining the streets. With all this competition, standards are high and service tends to come with a 'have a nice day' American smile. A slice of the US with a Welsh accent.

■ ■ AJ's Coffee House
City Road, Roath (029) 20451588

This café is the place to go to hang out with the 'in crowd' and wannabes. It's open daily serving tasty cappuccinos and an array of paninnis, main meals and baguettes. Growing popularity means it's a fight for a seat situation – rammed with office angels and students. Nifty disco balls hang from the ceiling serving as an unwanted 'morning after the night before' reminder. Not to worry – the caffeine should kick in soon.

■ ■ Atlantic Coffee Company
12 City Road, Roath (029) 2047 2300

Moving just slightly northwards, Atlantic is a Canadian coffee bar, and one that's definitely worth a visit. They've got an on-site roaster to toast, grind and froth your beans to perfection and serve a sublime cup. It's all very restful with wooden, high-back chairs and a homely, log cabin feel. If coffee's not enough check out the home baked treats and sarnies and excellent cookies and crumbles. There's also an array of cultured events like Salsa classes every Sunday, a library of books and local artwork on the walls. Taste it, experience it, enjoy it.

■ ■ Bar Europa
25 Castle Street (029) 2066 7776

Arty foreign students and random bohemian types make up the clientele at Europa. It used to be 'Friends' and has maintained the same vibe since the relaunch. A haunt for arty folk, thespians, poetry and film buffs congregating to congratulate each other on their new neckerchiefs and cigarette holders. The 'Happy Demons' poetry group is a must for the lyrically talented and a must-not for anyone feeling a bit fragile. Heartfelt, monotone warblings of unrequited love will tip you right over the edge. The Europa opens 'til late on selected nights serving obscure bottled beer and wicked desserts. Go on, let yourself go, you crazy people.

■ ■ Canadian Muffin Co.
High Street Arcade (029) 2023 2202

The best place in town for a nice bit of muff. They've got every conceivable flavour on offer, freshly baked and quite delicious. The service could be quicker if the staff weren't so busy gassing about last nights' conquests or their new nail extensions.

■ ■ Coffee Republic
St Johns Street (029) 2023 3902

The busiest coffee chain in town. The 'Republic' is modelled on a New York style coffee house and is just as scarily efficient. Really pretty decent, if you don't cringe at asking for 'coffee to flee', and the idea of corporate giants formulaically laying out the ideal place to chill out and rubbing their hands together in delight at their profit margins. If you haven't seen them all – on face value, Coffee Republic 'aint half bad.

■ ■ Coffee Republic
St Mary Street (029) 2039 5047

Exactly the same as the other one (see what we mean about formulaic?), except bigger and with an e-mail station with those fancy

Best Brekkie

It's ten in the morning, you have the odd rumble or two in your guts, though whether it's hunger or alcohol induced I'm not sure. So where's the best place to get one of those traditional English (or in our case Welsh) fry-ups? For the cheaper option in the centre, try the department store café deals. Debenhams and BHS offer a reasonable-sized breakfast to fill a gap for a mere £1.65, whilst Howells offer one at £1.85. If you're really looking for a feast and don't care about your wallet or your figure, try out Henrys' all day breakfast for £4.85. For those of you on the run, Bistro One will do you a breakfast roll for £2.50 or try a Servini's breakfast baguette from £2.20 (you can find them in the Wyndham Arcade) just mind how you go with the egg yoke. For those not in the town centre, Brava in Poncanna do a mean cooked brekkie for £4.45. For the very best in fry-ups, try out Ramons in Salisbury Road, Cathays, the best breakfast anywhere in the UK. £2-£3 will get you the biggest breakfast on a tray and leave you not wanting to eat for a week. If you're in the Bay and feeling famished and want the full monty (silver service treatment) then make your way to the Cutting Edge for brekkie, opening at the alarming time of 8am for a full English breakfast for £5.95 that'll fill a grand canyon.

Top Five Brekkies

Ramons
Cutting Edge
Henrys
Debenhams
Brava

flat screens. Access is a mere £2/hour, so they obviously hope to recoup the cost with the overpriced coffee. Upset the staff by bringing in your own flask of Nescafé. Or whisky.

■ ■ Coffee 1
Wood Street (029) 2066 4035

Newly established, chic coffee house near the train station. We're talking friendly staff and tasty coffee served the proper way. There are also loads of sweet options to enjoy as you chill in one of their comfy sofas. Treat yourself to the Chocolate Dippers (meant to be shared but hey...).

and cheap-tasting coffee. Mediocre in our book but if you're a coffee retard you won't notice the difference.

■ ■ Costa Coffee
Queen Street (029) 2066 5694

Cost a lot more like, and not that nice either. Another chain, so expect the usual gubbins. Bits of manufactured artwork, Costa radio

■ ■ Da Vinci
13 Quay Street (029) 2034 4044

A genuine Italian import – well, practically. Da Vinci offers a taste of Italy, from the coffee and décor, to the artwork on the walls, even

the staff are imported (they sound Italian anyway). One of the few places in town to serve Segafredo coffee at incredibly low prices (£1.30). Try one of the fresh insalate salads, paninnis or ciabatta sandwiches or itchy's personal favourite, the Parma ham salad for £3.50.

FT5K
Queens Arcade (029) 2034 0456

If you're wondering what the initials stand for it's, 'Feed The 5 Thousand', although I'd like to see what they could achieve given a couple of old mackerel, some breadcrumbs and a load of starving pilgrims. Somehow I don't think they'd cope. The place is reminiscent of an operating theatre, un-welcoming and uninspiring. There are plenty of stools dotted about but they only seem fit for giants and are very uncomfortable. I'd prefer to sit on a piece of wire or bamboo – at least it would be more stimulating. In my view, things don't improve with the food situation either. Criticism aside you can order your coffee in cute or sexy sizes, but don't push it and ask for orgasmic because they'd never understand.

Starbucks Coffee
(Bottom)Queen Street (029) 2037 3622
(Top) Queen Street (029) 2039 5845

Star Wars – The Empire Strikes Back or so it would seem. They started with one branch in Queen Street and now there's a skinny second and there are plans for more to come. The usual offerings from Starbucks can be enjoyed in both branches but they are a bit pricey.

Turquoise
Mermaid Quay (029) 2048 5566

A new concept food bar that's making its mark on the bay-side development of Mermaid Quay. Modern, swanky settings to enjoy a range of freshly prepared salads, wraps, noodles and baguettes to eat in or take away for the health conscious. Sound a bit too worthy? Well, there's only so many years you can live off a diet of burgers and Marlboro you know – it'll all catch up with you in the end. The wise will check out their details on the itchycardiff website and order online at their turquoisestop site.

RED DRAGON 103.2·97.4 FM **www.reddragonfm.co.uk**

clubs

www.itchycardiff.co.uk

■ ■ ■ Berlins Nightclub
5-9 Church Street (029) 20344468

R&B, garage and commercial dance galore. Is it, is it wicked? Do you really like it? Well, we'll leave that up to you. Hordes of loyal regulars religiously pack this cellar nightclub out, drawn presumably by the smoke, sweat and drinks promos. A line up of outrageous and bizarrely named nights make Berlin's a landmark in Cardiff's nightlife.

■ ■ ■ Clwb Ifor Bach
11 Womanby Street (029) 20232199

Clwb Ifor Bach rocks. Not in a sinister sweaty beards and air guitar way, but in an up for it, decent venue with attitude way. Music comes first with a range of superlative nights; Monday's Explosure showcases the best live bands, Tuesdays is Rock Scene, Wednesday plays host to Cardiff's number one student night Popscene, Thursday follows Monday's lead and weekends are a roadblock, with top-notch promoters, varied line-ups and massive crowds. Gone are the days when you had to be a member of Cymdeithas yr Iaith to get in here, but Clwb still remains very much the home of the Welsh speaker. In fact, demonstrating some kind of linguistic Welshness will go a long way towards helping you through the door on a hectic Saturday night.

Finger
tips

every friday
BERLINS

lock stock
& two smoking turntables

5 - 9 CHURCH STREET
CARDIFF. CF10 2BG

BERLINS
02920 344468

deliciously wicked

BERLINS EVERY SATURDAY NIGHT

■■■ Club Metropolitan
Bakers Row (029)20371549

If you've just hit your twenty fifth birthday and are teetering on the brink of an 'Oh my God, I'm nearly thirty' breakdown, this is the last place you should come. Stay home, rearrange your recipe books instead. This is your classic, dingy, alternative music venue, packed to the sweat soaked rafters with sullen looking indie kids. If you're not blessed with the kind of pallour that comes from years of lying face down on your bedroom floor listening to obscure devil-worshipping bands, they're just not going to take to you. It's Marilyn Manson t-shirts, eyeliner and steel toe caps all round – snarl, glare, don't break into a smile – welcome to the family.

■■■ Emporium Club
8-10 High Street (029) 20664577

Unlike the shonky clubs that desperately flog cheap drinks and cheesy chart to the masses to balance the books, the Emporium Club has steadfastly refused to stoop to the mainstream. It's a fairly basic shell, with different rooms offering different grooves – the emphasis here is strictly on the music. Eclectic as ever, the dance scene is in it's element here; US, UK and deep house, garage with UK garage and D'n'B sessions from Bullet Proof. Regular nights include, Funking Marvellous, L'America, Bionic and Vurto, to name a few. Of note is Tuesday's Hoochy Koochi student-fest – a rip roaring and perpetually rammed night out. Other nights see independent promoters and top DJs with storming sets – check out itchycardiff.co.uk for weekly listings.

top 5 for...
Pulling (Unfussy)
1. Liquid
2. Zeus
3. Latino's
4. Reds
5. Evolution

■ ■ The Edge
3-5 St Mary Street (029) 20303233

Riskily, they changed the name, the entertainment and the music policy, but The Edge still holds its cred and reputation throughout the city (the club, not the ageing U2 guitarist). Nestled between an array of bars and clubs, it's not your average drink 'til you puke kind of place, with a strikingly similar resemblance to an underground souk bar. Concentrating on r'n'b, garage and house, it attracts a mixed crowd of clubbers come the weekend, but all agree; this place is one of Cardiff's finest.

■ ■ Evolution Club
UCI Building, Cardiff Bay Leisure Village (029) 20464444

OK, so there's a rumour going around that some decent DJs might be taking to the decks at Evolution in the coming months. And if you're willing to risk your night out at the hands of a skanky carpeted, leisure complex club in the middle of nowhere, then go right ahead. Your time with us is done. There is nothing more we can do to help you.

Wednesday's student night is one thing, I mean, at least they've got an excuse. But other than rocking up alongside the city's academics for cheap drinks and a guaranteed snog, there's just no excuse. Do you hear us? Lasers, podium dancers and smoke machines, this is unadulterated stuck-in-the eighties hell. Live it large Cardiff, live it large. Don't bother checking itchycardiff.co.uk for line-ups.

■ ■ Flares
St Mary Street (029) 2023 5825

Welcome to seventies hell. Come forth in your slightly misjudged retro outfit and get-stuck into the discount alcopops. Stagger towards the dancefloor, burning people with your B&H on the way. If they dare complain, spin round, look hard and tell them they ming. 'Cos you, you're gorgeous – go on give it some on the dancefloor, show 'em what you're made of. Flail around wildly, periodically gyrate against the nearest table leg, pause briefly to fall over, pick yourself up again, then drunkenly lunge at unsuspecting passers by. Oh yes sir you can boogie...

EMPORIUM
NIGHTCLUB
www.emporium.pipz.com

L'AMERICA

PAST GUESTS: ROGER SANCHEZ, GOLDIE, DANNY RAMPLING, DIMITRI FROM PARIS, JOEY BELTRAM, PAUL VAN DYK, PAUL OAKENFOLD, LTJ BUKEM, TREVOR NELSON, JEREMY HEALY, 808 STATE, MR C, WU TANG CLAN, DREEM TEEM, BOBBI & STVE, PROPELLER HEADS, MASSIVE ATTACK, SCRATCH PERVERTS, GROOVERIDER, RONI SIZE, METAL HEADZ, TERRY FRANCIS, LISA LASHES, STEVE LANIER, CJ BOLLAND, RICH HTICHELL, RAEPH POWELL, AND MANY OTHERS

8-10 HIGH ST, CARDIFF
TEL:02920 664577

and your DISCO needs you. Flares is a drunken, youth club theme night on acid. The kind of place where you celebrate all five of your eighteenth birthdays and then never return again.

■ ■ ■ Liquid Nightclub
Imperial Gate, St Mary Street
(029) 20645464

Scrub up at the door, don latex gloves and a gown that shows your arse to the world, Liquid's 'Ritzy's for the new millennium' minimal chic is a bit like spending a pissed up night in your local A & E department. It's glaringly white and full of townie wide boys banging on about their 'kickin trainers' and the 'boss beats'. Though they won't actually be wearing trainers, because Liquid has one of those archaic door policies that also operates as an advanced warning for the commerical dance tunes that await you within. It's no jeans, no trainers, no style, setting you up for the kind of night your mother warned you about. From time to time, they manage to bag a decent DJ for the night and musically things improve (Graeme Park, Dave Pearce, Roger Sanchez and Trevor Nelson have all had a go) but no amount of quality mixing can compensate for the surprises in

store with some of the freaks we've met in here. Nights vary from the decent to the decrepit, so we'll tell you what's what on **itchycardiff.co.uk**

■ ■ ■ Jumpin' Jacks
Mill Lane, Town Centre (029)2022 5592

If there really was a Jumpin' Jack, he'd be wearing a luminous green shirt and shorts, with neon-flashing trainers. He'd offer cheap drinks to his mates, but only the saddest of desperadoes would bear his company for the night. Doubtless he'd reek of Old Spice, reckon that all the birds were gaggin' for it, and would like to 'ave it on a mad tip' come the weekend. Frankly, if he dropped dead tomorrow, it wouldn't be a day too soon. Move on.

■ ■ ■ Kiwis
21-27 Wyndham Arcade (029) 20229876

Not an Antipodean in sight. There are however the unlikely pulls of several hairy men with octopus hands accidentally finding their way up your skirt, bejewelled scary types lurking round the toilets and a location in an alleyway that doubles up as a urinal for passing drunkards. Kiwis offers a simple mix of booze, more booze and sport with no frills, no fuss and nobody with any taste within a four mile radius. There's one redeeming factor – a big screen for major sporting events. But notice I only said one. Happy hour runs daily from 11-7pm.

■■■ Las Iguanas
8-8A Mill Lane (029) 20226373

Slap bang in the Café Quarter of Mill Lane, blink and you'll miss the doors to this tiny club. Shake off the idea that this is a chain (there's a South American theme bar upstairs), cos it's not a bad little joint. It's tiny, let's be fair, but manages to maintain an intimate atmosphere. It's also so dark that you'll lose all your mates before the night is out, still it's handy for hiding from last weeks' beer-goggled misdemeanour. Rock up for happy hour 5-7.30 upstairs (2-4-1 cocktails), or take advantage of the meal deals between 12-6pm (2 course, £7), then stumble downstairs for chilled out tunes and house anthems.

■■■ Latino's
10 Mill Lane (029) 2064 5000

Wales's answer to Rio. Latino's is located upstairs in the Paparazzi building, formerly known as Continentals. Its latest incarnation is proving popular. Get some Salsa instruction on Mondays and shake your J-Lo inspired, collegen-injected fat rump to some cool, latino beats. There's a hilariously non-PC 'Ladies' night on Thursdays, with weekends serving up more of the same to a crowd of well-dressed, gyrating groovers.

■■■ M4 Soul Club
At the Riverbank Hotel
Despenser Street, Riverside
(01446) 746893

One of the last remaining original Northern Soul nights in the south. Just in case you've been stuck under a house music rock for years, Northern Soul is most definitely where it's at for soul grinders and sharp suit mods. The appeal remains pretty much the same as it was back in 60s Wigan, with classic slabs of Tamla soul forcing the stiffest of punters onto the dancefloor. Here music lovers from far and wide pack out the floor with fancy foot-work and kicks that'd put Jacko to shame. It generally attracts an older crowd, but if you've never heard real soul music (i.e. not those Levi's greatest hits albums), get on down, and don't be surprised if you become a convert for life. The M4 Soul Club is situated in the lower level of the hotel and is dark, sweaty and raw – just as it should be.

■■■ The Philharmonic
76-77 St Mary Street (029) 20230678

Flick through the papers

The Philly is long renowned for its Medic nights on Thursdays where doctors and nurses come out to play. And no, not in their uniforms. There's a bar upstairs, a club downstairs and a top-secret makeover on the cards. Watch this space.

■ ■ Reds

3 Churchill Way (029) 20641111

Use your straw as a makeshift Britney microphone and 'Hit me baby one more time'. Reds is pure tack at its finest. So if you think Judge Jules works for the Crown Court yet feel intimately acquainted with the complete works of SClub7, get yourself down here sharpish. This isn't somewhere to impress your out of town mates, nor somewhere you'd brag about being on the guest list for, but for a pissed up laugh that lasts 'til they chuck you out, it can't be beaten. Check out promo details at **itchycardiff.co.uk**

top 5 for...
Pulling (Fussy)

1. Emporium
2. Toucan
3. Clwb Ifor Bach
4. The Edge
5. Las Iguanas

■ ■ ■ Toucan Club

95 St Mary Street (029) 2037 2212

After several successful years at the Womanby Street location, Toucan has spread its wings and re-housed in St Mary Street. Fans of its old down-an-alley underground feel, will be pleased to know that it hasn't suffered too much at the hands of the high street effect. The line up is still quality. Check out the new sound system with a varied mix of jazz, world, funk, and hip hop. The likes of Wayne Gorbea, Papa Fall, Jack Costanzo not to mention live resident bands such as Quattro and Sol Latino all perform here. There's also the added bonus of local promoters such as Higher Learning and Rounda Records pulling in other top name DJs from the hip-hop circuit on Thursday nights. Come the weekend, the line-up places Cardiff on the funk map with the Mothership Convention, live bands and an up for it crowd. Toucan is doing its bit to push back the boundaries of clubbing, and with jazz on Sundays and popular unplugged music sessions on Wednesdays, it just goes to show that there are plenty of

The Toucan
New
Nest
St Mary Street
Cardiff
Open
16th Aug
live music club
chill out lounge
world cuisine
café bar
Phone: 20 372 212
sign up for free membership
members@toucanclub.co.uk
www.toucanclub.co.u

music lovers out there willing to support nights devoid of cheap alcopop bribes. You can subscribe as a member on their website or call the club.

■ ■ ■ Zeus
Greyfriars Road (029) 20377014

I lay in a pool of my own vomit. I don't know for how long, I just remember wishing it would all end; praying that the next breath would be my last. I could feel no pain, just a whiff of vodka Red Bull, turning my stomach over and over. I think I may have been unconscious for some time, the memories aren't as vivid as they were that night. It's like I dreamt it all, but I do remember clearly the sudden, shocking realisation that I wasn't dead. I was in Zeus, praying to the God of Gods that this would all end soon.

■ ■ ■ V2K
43-45 Queen Street (029) 20227717

A club the size of a small city. V2K is home to the masssively popular 'Enter The Dragon'

house night. A steady line-up of hot DJs take to the decks weekly. Past and present names include the likes of, Mario Picotto, Maurio Piu, Judge Jules, Tall Paul and Lisa Pin-Up.

■ ■ ■ Strip/ Lap/ Pole Dancing

■ ■ ■ The Fantasy Lounge
93 St Mar Street (029) 20382201/2

A year has passed since the Fantasy Lounge came to town amongst a tide of controversy and debate from the council. It's the only exclusive lap/pole dancing venue in the city centre, hence it's predominantly packed out with groups of lads and suits escaping the office for a quick fix. The club opens it's doors every night except Sunday from 9pm 'til 2am, but things kick off early on Friday when the dancing starts at 2pm and goes on 'til 2am and 8pm 'til 3am Saturday. Full of fannies (i.e. the punters).

Keri (+mates), 21+, Single mum

OK, so when the kids are at home, I take it you like a drink?
Yes! (in unison, shrieking). Prince of Wales
And then onto a club?
(more shrieking). Evolution!
Sshh now. And your favourite restaurant?
Bar Med, it's got a really happy atmosphere
So what's great about Cardiff?
The men! THE MEN!
And the worst?
Too bloody far from the valleys! (howling)

club listings

For more up-to-date reviews, previews and listings check www.itchycardiff.co.uk

All listings details are subject to change at short notice, and should therefore be used as a guide only.

Club	Name of night	Music	Door tax	Hours	Dress code	Drinks offers
MONDAY						
Clwb Ifor Bach	Explosure	Live bands	£3	9-2am	-	-
Fantasy Lounge	Lap/Pole dancing	–		9-2am	Smart casual	-
Flares	Student night	70s disco	Free	7-2am	No trainers	£1.50 select drinks
Liquid	Student night	Dance/Party	£3/£2 NUS	9.30-2am	No dress code	£1.50 selected
Latinos	Salsa night	Salsa/disco	£4.50/£3.50 NUS	7-1am	No dress code	-
Club X/cafebar	Chill-out	Chart	Free	6pm-11pm	-	£1 drinks all night
Exit Club	–	Chart	£1.50/£3	7.30-2am	-	-
TUESDAY						
Clwb Ifor Bach	Rock Inferno	Rock bands	£3	9-2am	-	-
Club Metropolitan	Offya Face	Rap/ska/punk	£2.50 (£1.50)	9-2am	-	-
Emporium	Hoochy Koochi	Disco 70s/80s	£2B410/£3	9.30-2am	-	£1-£1.50 selected
Fantasy Lounge	Lap/Pole	-		9-am	-	-
Flares	Student night	Disco 70s	Free	7-2am	-	£1.50 selected
Latinos	Tutti Frutti	Chart	Free B4 11pm, £1 after. £3 NUS	9-2am	-	£1 selected drinks
Toucan Club	Live bands	Live bands	£2 NUS/£3	7-2am	-	-
Zeus	Bonk night	Student night (chart)	£2.50 B4 10.30 (£1 NUS), £3.50 after (£3 NUS)	9-2am	-	£1 selected drinks
Club X/cafebar	Chill-out	Chart	Free	6pm-11pm	-	-
Exit Club		Chart	£1.50 / £3	7.30-2am	-	-
WEDNESDAY						
Berlins	Cardiff Uncovered	R&B, Garage	£1, £2, £3	8-2am	-	£1.50 selected
Clwb Ifor Bach	Popscene/ Cheesy club	Chart, breaks funk, disco	£3/£2.50 NUS	9.30-2am	-	£1 bottle
Evolution	Student night	Chart/trnce/hs	£4, £3 NUS/Epic	9.30-2am	No sportswear	£1 selected drinks
Fantasy Lounge	Lap/Pole dancing	-		9-2am	Smart	-
Flares	Boggie Box	Karaoke/disco	Free	7-2am	-	2-4-1 offers
Liquid	Student night	Comm. chart	£2-£5	9.30-2am	Smart trainers	Select bottle offs.
Jumping Jacks	Band night	Rock/alt.		9-2am	-	-
Kiwis	DJ night	Cheesy chart	£2-£4	10-2am	No toecaps	Varying offers
Reds	Student night	Cheesy chart	£3 / £2 itchy	9-2am	-	£1 bottle offers
Toucan Club	Accoustic session	Live sets	£2/£3 NUS	7-2am	-	-
V2K	VFM	Commercial		9-2am	-	70p/pint
Club X	Uni-sex	Chart/house	£1 NUS/£3 other	10-2am	-	£1 drinks
Exit	-	Chart	£1.50/£3	7.30-2am	-	Berlins
THURSDAY						
Berlins	R&B, Garage		£1,£2, £3	-	8-2am	-	£1.50 selected
Clwb Ifor Bach	Calico Wall	Alt./bands	-	10-2am	-	£1 Carslberg

Club	Name of night	Music	Door tax	Hours	Dress code	Drinks offers
Club Metropolitan	Spellbound	Indie/alt	£2.50 (£1.50)	9-2am	-	£1 pints
Evolution	Vodka Thursday	Chart/mix	£3 (£1)	9.30-2am	-	50p flav. vodka
Fantasy lounge	Lap/Pole dancing	-	-	9-2am	Smart	-
Flares	Angels	70s/disco	Free	7-2am	-	Various
Liquid	Soul Power	R&B, garage	£4/£1	9.30-2am	Smart casual	-
Kiwis	DJ night	Chart/mix	£2-£4	10-2am	No toecaps	Various
Latinos	Medic night	Chart/mix	£3/£2 NUS	9-2am	-	£1.50 selected
Reds	-	Cheese/karke.	£3	9-2am	-	Various
Toucan Club	-	Hip hop/beats	£2/£3 NUS	7-2am	-	-
Zeus	Disco Inferno	70s disco	£3/£4	9-2am	-	Various
Exit		Chart/mix	£1.50/ £3	7.30-2am		

FRIDAY

Club	Name of night	Music	Door tax	Hours	Dress code	Drinks offers
Berlins	Lock, stock...	R&B/garage	£1/£4	8-2am	No sportswear	HHour 'til 11
Clwb Ifor Bach	Variable	Hip hop, house	£6	10-2.30am	-	-
Club Metropolitan	Chaos	Indie/alt.	£3	9-2am	-	Vodbull jug £6
Emporium	DJ Promoters	Grge, D'nb	£5-£12	10-4am	Smart casual	-
Evolution	R-O-A-R	Hard house	£12 (£10)	10-5am	-	-
Fantasy Lounge	Lap/Pole dancing	-	-	2pm-2am	Smart	-
Flares	Ultimate Party	70s/chart	£2 after 10.30pm	7-2am	Smart, 21s+	-
Liquid	Drink 4 free	Variable	£5 B4 11pm	9.30-2am	Smart, 20s+	-
Jumpin Jacks	DJ Night	Cheesy chart	-	7-2am	Smart	-
Kiwis	DJ Night	Cheesy chart	£2-£4	10-2am	No toecaps	-
Las Iguanas	Cool House	US house	free	8-2am	Smart	-
Latino's	Party night	Chart/mix	£5	9-2.30am	Smart, 21s+	-
Reds	Party night	Cheesy chart	£3-£4	9-2am	Smart	-
Toucan Club	Mothership Convention	Funk, live bands	£5-£10	7-2am	-	-
Zeus	Bar 150	Chart/mix	£3	9.30-3am	Smart	-
V2K	Enter The Dragon	House	£8-£12, NUS £8	10-6am	No attitude (!)	HHour 10-11pm
Club X	Foreplay	House	£4 (3)	10-3am	Smart casual	£1.50 selected
Exit	-	Chart/mix	£2-£3	7.30-2am	Smart casual	

SATURDAY

Club	Name of night	Music	Door tax	Hours	Dress code	Drinks offers
Berlins	Deliciously Wicked	UK grge/dance	£1-£4	8-2am	No sportswear	£1.50 drinks
Clwb Ifor Bach	Variable	Alt/live bands	£5	10-2.30am	-	-
Metros	Variable	Chunky indie		9-3am	-	-
Emporium	Variable	Prog/grg/rmb	£5-£12	10-4am	No sportswear	-
Evolution	Evolution night	Hse/trnce/chrt	£6, £5 epic	9.30-4am	Smart, 20+	-
Fantasy Lounge	Lap/Pole dancing	-	-	8-2am	Smart	-
Flares	The Ultimate Party	70s disco	£2 after 10.30pm	7-2am	Smart, 21+	-
Liquid	Variable	Variable	£6	9.30-3am	Smart, 21+	-
Jumpin Jacks	DJ Night	Chart/mix	-	7-2am	Smart casual	-
Kiwis	DJ Night	Chart/mix	£2-£4	10-2am	Smart	-
Las Iguanas	Hombu	Breaks/house	Free	8-2am	Smart	-
Latinos	Party night	Chart/mix	£7	9-2.30am	Smart, 21+	-
Reds	Party night	Cheesy chart	£3-£4	9-3am	Smart, 21+	-
Toucan Club	Club Latino	World /live	£5-£10	7-2am	-	-
Zeus	Innocent	Dnce/grge	£3-£4	9.30-3am	Smart, 19+	-
V2K	Urban Groove	Rn'b, UK grge	£6 (£3/fly)	9-4am	No trainers	£1.50 HHour 9-11
Club X	-	Hard house	£5-£7	10-4am	-	-
Exit	-	Chart/mix	£2-£3	7.30-2am	-	

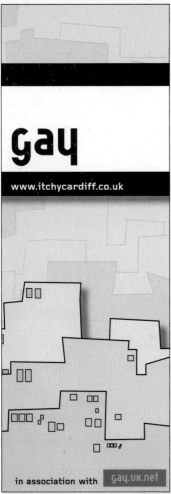

gay

www.itchycardiff.co.uk

Welcome to Cool Cymru. Since the rebirth of the word cool and its intimate attachment to Cardiff, this town has become an almost re-tox city. Cardiff queers have taken the sheep home with 'em and given it a darn good dip... now that animal is a beast worthy of any metropolitan scene.

Pubs

Kings Cross
Mill Lane (029) 2064 9891

Located in the heart of the European-style cafe piazza quarter, the 'world famous' (make your own mind up about that tag line...) Kings Cross has been serving the gay community for over 25 years. Complete with terrace on a tree-lined street, where you can eat or drink al fresco, the Kings has always been popular with the boys and girls, but note it's men-only on Thursdays.

Golden Cross
283 Hayes Bridge Road (029) 2039 4556

Traditional boozer in a listed building that boasts many artistic features, including carved wooden pillars and a huge mosaic-tiled picture of Cardiff Castle. Run by twins Gareth and Darren (voted best shag of the year in the Gay Wales Fairy Awards 1999), the Golden also serves up some of the finest grub found in any pub – with lashings of home cooked goodies served daily. It's advisable to book for Sunday lunch. Every Monday, Tuesday, Wednesday and Thursday buy four pints and get a fifth free. Watch out for various cabaret nights. Every Saturday night is handbag night. Sunday night is camp music, camp bar staff and camp prices.

Clubs

Exit Club

48 Charles Street (029) 2064 0102

The door price is shamefully low at just £1.50 most nights, so you don't need an excuse to come here. A cabaret-free zone, relying more on heavily touted drinks promotions. Suits us – they know how to turn

The Edge

Charles Street (029) 2040 0876

Chill-out space connected to the growing Club X night spot. Open daily from 6pm serving up £1 drinks and a playful atmosphere. Highly popular pre-club bar and chill-out zone.

the punters on – get 'em pissed so they won't care about the surroundings.
Open 'til 2am every night apart from Sunday when the bar closes at 12.30am.

■ ■ Club X
Charles Street (029) 2040 0876
The biggest gay club in Wales has had yet another face-lift. Newly extended beer garden, games room, pool room and balcony area. Adjoined to The Edge cafe bar so you can chill out or alternatively shake your bod to the hard house dished up on 'Uni-sex Wednesday' or 'Foreplay Friday'. Hard house, NU-NRG and retro-disco make up the music menu (so nothing new there then) .
Weds 10-2am, Fri 10-3am, Sat 10-4am, Sun 9.30-1am
Weds £1 with NUS card/£2.50 all others, Fri £3, Sat £5. Free on Sun; entry through The Edge.

Geraint & Gareth, 21/22, Young profs.

OK, so where's best for a quick pint?
Bar 38 is usually pretty decent of a night
Warming you up for where?
Clwb Ifor Bach is always kicking
True, true. How about restaurants?
Wetherspoons
Uh, classy. I am of course joking. Best thing about Cardiff?
The variety of people in the city
And the worst?
Townies on the lash
You get what you pay for you know...

■ ■ Spa

■ ■ Locker Room Health Spa
50 Charles Street (029) 2022 0388
Health Spa my arse, but as Salt 'n' Pepa said, 'it's good and natural', so I guess a bit of what you fancy does you and your ego a lot of good. A hugely popular sauna with extensive facilities including buffet area, Swiss sauna, steam rooms, jacuzzi, TV lounge, video lounge and restroom. Mary Whitehouse wouldn't approve.
Sun-Fri 1pm-11pm, last entry 10pm, Sat 1pm-6am Sunday.
£2 annual membership/£1 day membership, £10 admission.

RED DRAGON 103.2-97.4 FM **www.reddragonfm.co.uk**

shopping

www.itchycardiff.co.uk

■■ Shopping Centres

■■ Capitol Centre
Queen Street (029) 2022 3683

Watch the crowds stream forth, transfixed by the glimmer of Capitol's glass facade, like lambs to the retail slaughter. Not only does this centre offer a whole host of places to flash your plastic under one roof, it's also the only shopping centre in the capital to offer on-site parking. The recent refurb has produced a state of the art retail experience bringing together independent retailers and high street chains. You'll find the likes of Benetton, Karen Millen and Oasis rubbing shoulders with Hudson & Hudson and Cinderellas. And if clothes aren't high on your list of priorities you can stock up your CD collection at Virgin Megastore, pick up a novel gift at the Gadget Shop or review your credit situation over coffee in Cafe Caribe.
Mon-Wed, Fri/Sat 9-6pm, Thu 9-7pm,
Sun 11-5pm

■■ Queens Arcade
**Queens Street/ Johns Street
(029) 2022 3581**

Not to be confused with the St Davids Centre which merges with it. This is a pretty average arcade and the most fun you can have is probably running down the up escalator, or you know, running up the down escalator. Don't let us influence your decision though; feel free to cause havoc in any way you see fit. Within the two floors you'll find the perpetually evil Disney Store, luring innocent children into its sinister depths and a few decent interiors shops.
Mon-Sat 8.30-6pm, Thu 8.30-8pm,
Sun 11-5pm

■ ■ St Davids
Queen Street (029) 2039 6041

A big arcade with big retailers. Rock up for M&S, BHS, Boots, Woolworths and Debenhams. All your dull, practical shopping needs fulfilled under the one roof. Forgive me for my blatant lack of enthusiasm.

Mon-Wed 8.30-6.30, Thu 8.30-8, Fri-Sat 8.30-6.30, Sun 11-5

■ ■ McArthur Glen Designer Outlet
Bridgend (01656) 665 700

Situated just off the M4 (Junction 36) this shopping complex is like a car boot sale at

the Beckhams. Designer garms at knocked down prices and a stampede of shoppers in search of bargains. You'll find Ben Sherman, Nike, CK Jeans, Timberland and Elle amongst the rails and constant promotions and events. Hell, even Bob the Builder has made an appearance here – it's all glamour. And it's open 'til 8pm every night during the week.

Mon-Fri 10-8, Sat 10-6, Sun 11-5

■ ■ Department Stores

■ ■ Howells
St Mary Street (029) 2023 1055

Howells is massive; once you've found you way in, it's a bit like being in the crystal maz – confusing, exhausting and full of mystica ly dressed bald men. If you've been traipsin round town all day and still haven't foun what you want, this place houses the lo There's a quality menswear line-up wit Nicole Farhi, DKNY and Linea, plenty for gir and more household items than you coul ever need. Worth a look in itself is the foo hall – packed with biscuits, specialty coffee cheese, handmade chocolates and deli stuf Check out the range of specialty beers 'Slap & Tickle', 'Old Gee Spot', 'Brew 69' an 'Sweet F.A'. Hilarious.

Mon-Wed, Fri & Sat 9-6pm, Thurs 9-8pn Tues 9.30-6pm, Sun 10-5.30pm

■ ■ David Morgans
The Hayes (029) 2022 1011

A proper old timer of a department store this place has been here forever. You'll nee an orienteering kit to find your way round it's jammed with everything from clothe and homeware, to cards and countless gi ideas. The place tends to be packed wit families on day trips so it's pretty much case of dodge the sulking toddler. Not for th faint-hearted. Escape to the roof terrace caf and hope they don't follow you.

Mon & Wed, Fri 9-5.30pm, Tues 9.30-5.30pn Thurs 9pm-8pm, Sat 9-6pm, openin Sundays, soon...

■ ■ BHS
0-54 Queen Street (029) 2039 0167

remember coming to BHS with my gran nd it was usually fun 'cos I used to get weets from the pic 'n' mix counter whilst he bought her baggy pants. I'm older now. rekkie sets you back a mere £1.65 which is redeeming feature.

Mon-Wed 9-5.30pm, Thurs 9-8pm, Fri& Sat 9- pm, Sun 11-5pm

■ ■ Debenhams
St Davids Arcade (029) 2039 9789

Worth a mention for their 'Designers at Debenhams' range – film star style at data entry prices. Other than that you'll find the usual perfume, cosmetics, homeware and clothes for the whole family.

Mon, Wed, Fri, Sat 9-6, Tue 9.30-6, Thu 9-8, Sun 11-5

■ ■ Marks & Spencers
Queen Street (029) 2037 8211

Need to impress your new beau with your xtraordinary culinary genius? Look no fur- her – just remember to peel off the label. Also worth checking out are the men's suits, which with their Italian cut and style, look a hell of a ot more expensive than they really are.

Mon-Wed 9-6pm, Thu-Fri 8.30-8pm, Sat 8.30- pm, Sun 10.30-5pm

■ ■ Shopping Areas

■ ■ Cardiff Central Markets
Off St Mary Street and The Hayes

There are over fifty stalls to browse under one Victorian, glass roof. This is a good place to come for bargain fruit and veg, or to check out the second hand and bric-a-brac stalls. One word of warning though – don't pass the pet stand – rather than cute scampering kittens begging you to take them home, you'll find something far more sinister. Dejected, manky looking animals who seem to have entirely given up on the concept of anyone ever rescuing them from their market hell. Utterly tragic.

■ ■ The Arcades

Ask any Cardiff shopper worth their deconstructed denims where the ultimate in Cardiff shopping can be found and they'll pack you off here. So whether you're a local or a visitor read on for some of the Welsh capital's finest.

The main arcades can be reached from St Johns Street, High St, Duke St or St Mary Street. Each arcade is home to an array of independent shops offering bits 'n' bobs for the home and top-notch fashion.

Check out the **High Street** and **Duke Street** arcades for a fetish fumble in Eccentrixs, or cool indie clothes brands Pussy Galore and Drooghi. Budding Imelda Marcos's will be happy in Buzz and homebodies will spend a small fortune in Nice interiors.

Cross the road and head down the **Castle Arcade**. Get se-juiced by a health-kick beverage at the Organic Juice Company. As for the rest there's Constantinou for bargain hair-cuts, Gokyo for men's clothes and Chessman for ladies. Take a sharp exit into the DJ record shop and get the latest vinyl releases to add to your collection.

If you're still standing at this point, walk back to **St Mary Street** and towards the bus station to find the **Morgan** and **Royal Arcades**. Morgan's is home to baggy skate-wear store Route One as well as Woodies Emporium – replace that old Ralph Lauren shirt townie boys. You'll also find The Villiers Gallery, Blackwells book shop and a myriad of ethnic items at One World Trading.

Go back out onto St Mary Street and turn left into the **Royal Arcade.** Refuel at Fresh with their excellent baguettes, then move on to Room for 'Look how well travelled I am' furniture. Plus a lot more that we can't even hope to include here – get browsing.

Other arcades not to be missed out are the **Oxford Arcade** off the Hayes and the **Dominions** and **Andrews Arcades** off Queen Street. Shop 'til you drop.

■ ■ ■ Queens Street

Queens Street is one of Cardiff's main shopping areas, playing host to all the high street chains. You know the score, we're talking Top Shop, M&S, River Island, WHSmith, Dixons – need we continue?

■ ■ ■ Menswear

■ ■ ■ Chessman
10-14 Castle Arcade (029) 2025 6140
There are too many designer labels here to mention – so we won't. Just rest assured there's ample opportunity to flex your plastic.

■ ■ ■ Drooghi
High Street Arcade (029) 2023 0332
Their own brand 'Rather Not Say' T-shirts, are walking out of the shop faster than they can manage to restock. The likes of James Dean Bradfield from the Manics and Ant & Dec are big fans – we suspect you will be too.

■ ■ ■ Gokyo
35 Castle Arcade (029) 2025 6148
Smart, street-style from Stussy, Duffer, Triple Five, Diesel and G Star.

it's time to shop baby.

C A R D I F F ' S

high street/duke street arcades and castle arcade

THE PLACE FOR COOL SHOPPING.

T: 02920342096

■ ■ ■ Women's Clothes

■ ■ ■ Eccentrixs
St Mary Street (029) 2022 3037
Outrageous footwear – from funky, hardcore boots and tiny stilettos, to flip-flops and those old skool Spice Girl shoes favoured by Italian teenage girls.

■ ■ ■ Oasis
Capital Shopping Centre, Queens Street (029) 2023 1791
(In Howells Dep Store) 14 St Mary Street (029) 2023 1055
Weekend shopping is like going to war and Oasis is the front line, packed come Saturday afternoon with panic-stricken girls on a perfect outfit mission. Oasis offers designer style at affordable prices, a fast enough turnover to ensure you don't end up in the same hipsters as every other girl in your local and a myriad of up-to-the-minute shoes and accessories. Everything you could ever need. Frankly I'd move in if only they'd let me.

■ ■ ■ Pussy Galore
High St Arcade (029) 2031 2400
Unique, glamourous clothes for special occasions. This is one of Cardiff's best independent clothes shops – always packed with pre-big night out groups of girls trying on low cut tops and classy dresses.

■ ■ ■ Gentle Folk
Duke St Arcade (029) 2023 2344
Status Quo heaven. Whatever you want, whatever you like. Hit the denim scene here – their own brand sells like hotcakes. It's unisex, and I like it, I like it, I like it, I liiiiiiiiike it, liiiiiiike it, here we gooooooo, rockin' all over the world. Repeat to fade(d) denim.

■ ■ ■ Unisex Clothes Shops

■ ■ ■ Barkers
1-5 Castle Arcade (St Mary Street) (029) 2037 1491
Unisex store stocking flared trousers, hooded tops, shirts and stylised American retro wear. They also sell those 'made in Wales, fondle with care' t-shirts for patriotic National obsessives.

IT'S THE MD

■■ Floyds
23 High Street (029) 2039 8757
The discerning dressers' independent clothes shop. Floyds specialises in denim, leather and more formal items for day or night. It's funky, chunky and attracts no monkeys.

■■ Hobos
26 High Street Arcade (029) 2034 1188
Second hand clothes for 50s, 60s and 70s dudes. Check out their massive range of flares, shirts, tank tops and leather jackets. Your disco needs you – the least you can do is look the part.

■■ I-Claudius
Castle Arcade (029) 2022 2215
Yeah baby yeah, the widest flares in town primed for purchase by wannabe disco chicks. This is the kind of shop you'll lose hours in just rummaging around. Take a two-hour lunch and make the most of it.

■■ Road
4-6 High Street Arcade (029) 2022 8056
A newcomer to the High Street Arcade and a very welcome one. Road sells own brand

clothing, naughty girl Custard tops with matching bags, excellent denim stuff and Go Vicinity Jeans. They also stock the Acid Casuals range and other hip, local print brands.

■■ WRC
8-10 High Street (029) 2022 7576
Remember going down the park on a Friday night for your weekly bottle of Strongbow? You and your eight mates all wearing iden-tikit Happy Mondays t-shirts and stonewashed jeans? Well shopping here is like embracing the adult equivalent – the same dull labels that are wasting space in everyone elses wardrobe as well as your own. If you want to blend in with the crowd, shop here.

■■ Surf & Outdoor Pursuits

■■ City Surf
27 Castle Arcade (029) 2034 2068
With Cardiff being internationally renowned for its beaches this surf wear emporium is naturally packed with punters. Plenty of clothes and hardware for surf, snow and skaters and anyone else that likes to say 'dude' a lot.

■■ Fat Face
9-11 High Street Arcade (029) 2066 4383
Easy wear clothes with that 'lived-in' feel. Great selection of fleeces, loads of cool t-shirts, cropped trousers, underwear, sandals, trainers, keyrings, wallets and bags.

SHOW HIM YOU'RE NOT INTIMIDATED

■ ■ ■ Freerider Stores (Spray)
Queens Arcade (029) 2023 1338

A prime spot for the Cardiff surf, skate and snow fraternity, Spray carries an eclectic range of clothing and hardware. Popular clothing brands include Rusty and the Coca-Cola range, it's also a good place to pick up some decent equipment and get professional advice on skate 'n' snow stuff. Watch out for the staff gettin 'jiggy' with the tunes on the in-store decks.

■ ■ ■ Freespirit
St. Johns Street (029) 2022 8032

New addition to the burgeoning sport and outdoor pursuits shopping scene. Packed with slightly too neat looking fourteen year old boys who've clearly never seen a wave in their life.
Mon-Sat 9-6pm, Thurs 9-8pm, Sun 10.30-5pm

■ ■ ■ Mambo
3-5 High Street Arcade (029) 2064 1983

A shop with a very laid back vibe – in fact you feel you could almost haggle (almost I said, don't try it). They stock Globe and

Airwalk trainers as well as the Mambo range. Mon-Thur 10-5.30pm, Fri & Sat 10-6pm, Sun 12-4pm

■ ■ Music Shops

■ ■ ■ The DJ Recordshop.com
30 Castle Arcade (029) 2091 1099

Newly revamped two-storey emporium of super cool vinyl. If you're into your tunes in a big way then this is the place to come and stock up. Wall to wall vinyl, decks to sample your prospective choices on and every genre under the sun, particularly garage, house, funk, progressive mixes and hip-hop. Check out the attached café Space and dream about those new decks and fast faders from the DJ hardware selection upstairs.
Mon-Sat 10-5.30pm, closed Sunday

■ ■ ■ Catapult 100% Vinyl
22 High Street Arcade (029) 2022 8990

The Mecca for Cardiff DJs (we're assuming it's not for those with mobile discos and names like Wayne). There's a wide range of tunes and 'in the know' staff, making this an essential

JUST KEEP SMILING AT HIM

top-off for any DJ worth his 12 inches.
Mon-Sat 10-6pm, closed Sunday

▮▮ Kellys Records
222 Central Market (029) 2037 7355
Second-hand emporium of music and
audio-visual stuff. There's a plethora of
albums and tapes to wade through, you
could lose days in here, just watch out for
Elvis lurking in the corner.

▮▮ Spillers Records
36 The Hayes (029) 2022 4905
Claims to be the oldest music shop in the
world (it says so on the billboard so it must
be true) but the music content is bang up to
date. You can pick up everything from the
left side of life, from Cuban collectives to
New York hardcore. They also stock the best
range of Northern Soul in town. Well worth
a visit.

▮▮ D'Vinyl Records
Mackintosh place (029) 2049 4998
Another second hand joint situated in Roath
out of town but worth the trip. It has that

charity shop feel, all a bit jumbled and baf-
fling. There's bargains to be had – just be
prepared to work your way through a verita-
ble pop music hall of fame to find them.

▮▮ Virgin Megastore
7-9 Capitol Arcade (029) 2038 8273
Massive music store slap bang in the town
centre. There's CDs, DVDs, games, videos and
regular band signing sessions. The lower
floor is dedicated to albums and chart with
vinyl releases and specialist mags. Check out
the second level for rare stuff and the comprehensive selection of material by Welsh
artists.

▮▮ HMV
51 Queen Street (029) 2022 7147
High street music and entertainment store
offering a wide range of chart music, games,
DVDs and our guides of course. They also
stock a fair range of vinyl for you to check
out on their instore decks.

▮▮ MVC
29 – 31 The Hayes (029) 2039 4650
CDs, DVDs, games and videos at discount
prices with a freely available membership
card. Open 'til 8pm daily.

▮▮ Book Shops

▮▮ BookSale
17 Church Street (029) 2022 8422
Bargain books and other reading material
sold at knock down prices.

BEWARE OF THE VOICES. FOR CAREER ADVICE WORTH LISTENING TO,
INCLUDING **HELP** WITH **INTERVIEWS**, VISIT monster.co.uk

Page 7
www.itchyleeds.co.uk

■ ■ ■ Oriel Book Shop
18-19 High Street (029) 20395548

The best Welsh book shop in town. Also stocks all kinds of professional looking stationary – ideal for those blagging letters of complaint to Marlboro.

■ ■ ■ Troutmark Books
41-43 Castle Arcade (029) 2038 2814

No old trout in here, just aisles of second hand books and hundreds of comics. Not to be confused with Trout Bookmarks – an altogether different kind of amphibian page-keeper.

■ ■ ■ Waterstone's
2a The Hayes (029) 2066 5606
18-20 Hills Street (029) 2022 2723

The reigning King of Cardiff bookland. Wall to wall fiction, culture, arts and city guides including this one – itchy Cardiff. And itchy Bristol. And itchy London, itchy Cambridge, itchy Liverpool, itchy Leeds, itchy Sheffield, itchy Oxford, itchy Edinburgh, itchy Birmingham, itchy ... you get the picture.

■ ■ ■ Blackwells Books
13-17 Royal Arcade (029) 2039 5036

Don't be deceived by the outside, this book shop is massive. The staff are welcoming and will help you find whatever you're looking for. With a huge range of titles they're bound to have what you're looking for – especially if you're looking for academic texts. Enough to induce instant exam stress, even if education is nothing but a repressed and distant memory.

■ ■ ■ Lears Bargain Books
13-17 Royal Arcade (029) 2039 5036

Bargain book extravaganza backing onto Blackwells bookshop.

!	📄	📎	From	Subject
	✉		itchycity.co.uk	Weekend offers to your inbox

■■ WH Smith
Queen Street (029) 2039 0088
Comprehensive store selling books, periodicals, stationery and board games.

■■ Deck out Your Pad

■■ Habitat
**9-11 The Hayes Building, The Hayes
(029) 2022 8811**
Does this shop need explaining? Stockists of all that's minimal, chic and sophisticated. Oh yeah, and it's quite pricey too.

■■ Melin Tregwynt - Woollen Mill
Royal Arcade (029) 2022 4997
Contemporary throw-overs, rugs and accesories to smarten your home with. All the fabrics are woven from Welsh wool. Fantastic in every way.

■■ Nice
15 High Street Arcade (029) 2064 5181
No relation to the biscuit but it does stock tons of sweet bits 'n' bobs to turn your dodgy but cheap flat into something a bit more liveable.

■■ Other Cool Shops

■■ Forbidden Planet
5 Duke Street (029) 2022 8885
They've got everything for the comic, horror, sci-fi, video, and games freak. So come on down – move away from the TV screen and put the joystick away.

■■ The Gadget Shop
**The Capital Shopping Centre
(029) 2039 4355**
Socks, hankie three-packs, novelty choco-

lates – it's all over now. Gadget Shop offers something a bit different when it comes to that awkward birthday gift. They also stock this fine, beautiful title, bound by the fair hands of virgins.

■ ■ ■ Johnnies Condom Shop
Castle Arcade (029) 2040 6969

Use your imagination, otherwise the assistant will help you and be forced to give you demonstrations. It's as silly as you like; furry handcuffs, whips, after dinner nipples, chocolate penises or pasta willies. Better than the real thing.

■ ■ ■ Welsh Crafts
Castle Street (029) 2034 3038

Tourists flock to this shop to buy a taste of Wales, it's cameras at dawn, so take some shades to avert the intermittent flash bulbs. All this paparazzi action appears to be on

account of the worlds largest love spoon – although I'm still not quite sure exactly what one is. Buy a little piece of Wales and rejoice.

■ ■ ■ Withit
12 Morgan Arcade (029) 2066 7970

Novelty shop that sells funny T-shirts, mugs, cards and 'baccy tins – you get the gist. Though of course, when we say funny, we mean it in the loosest possible Royal Variety on ITV for the family sense of the word.

■ ■ ■ WRU Official Shop
Wood Street (029) 2023 2700

Unsurprisingly stocks endless Welsh rugby regalia. Rugby jerseys, sweaters, fleeces, mugs (the drinking kind) and anything with a Welsh flag on it. If you're a rugby fan this will be your second home (after the pub, obviously).

Oi! You! Get writing, now!

So you reckon you can do better do you? Oh I get it, sitting there, all blasé, telling all your mates what a wordsmith you are. Yeah, you could've been a novelist if you really wanted to – apparently – if you could be arsed to get off your sedentary and frankly rather large arse and scrawl a few choice words. Well, prove it.

We're looking for writers for itchycardiff.co.uk for experts in every area – music, clubs, restaurants, bars, the arts – the whole shebang. Whatever your speciality, if you'd like to get involved, contact us at **cardiffwriters@itchymedia.co.uk** with a sample of either a venue review or something entertaining you've written, we'll have a read through, and get in touch.

itchy sms @
www.itchycardiff.co.uk

WHATEVER TURNS YOU ON *Virgin* megastores

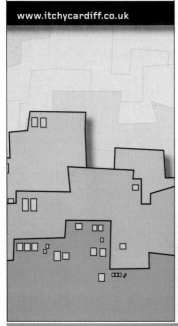

entertainment

www.itchycardiff.co.uk

Entertainment Centres

Atlantic Wharf Leisure Village
Hemmingway Road, Cardiff Bay
(029) 2088 8990

You'll have no problem finding a vast array of pubs, clubs, cinema screens and bowling alleys, but to find them all under one roof is a definite bonus. The leisure complex in Atlantic Wharf offers just that – UCI 12-screen cinema, Hollywood Bowling alley, Rosies and Old Orleans. It's also home to the Red Dragon Radio station and to top it off the complex has its own club, Evolution, the biggest in Cardiff. See club section for review.

The Millennium Plaza
Wood Street

This spanking new complex is situated in front of the Millennium Stadium and due to open later in 2001. Log onto www.itchycardiff.co.uk for up-to-date details of what's going on.

Millennium Waterfront
Cardiff Bay (029) 2022 7281

Mermaid Quay is fast developing, heralding a new look Cardiff. New ventures are always being unveiled – the most recent being the Glee Comedy Club and several new restau-

rants. Round these parts sight-seeing is top of the agenda with the Norwegian Church, Visitors Centre, Techniquest and loads of other things you're supposed to show your visiting aunties.

■ ■ Cinemas

■ ■ Chapter Arts Centre
Market Road, Canton (029) 2030 4400
Foreign, Welsh and British films you might otherwise never see. Look out for seasons and special events. Splendid.

■ ■ Galaxy Globe
Albany Road (029) 2049 5065
New Indian specialists in one of the city's oldest surviving cinemas. This is the place for all of those hard to find Bollywood classics. Outstanding.

■ ■ Monico Twin Cinemas
Pantbach Road (029) 2069 3426
If you fancy watching a flick away from the hustle and bustle of the town centre, then this is the place to go. Marvellous.

■ ■ Ster Century Cinemas
**Millennium Plaza, Town Centre
(029) 2055 0500**
New addition to the city centre housed within the Millennium Plaza leisure complex, next to the Millennium Stadium. Fantastic.

■ ■ UCI
**Atlantic Wharf, Cardiff Bay
(029) 2088 8990**
12 screens showing all the latest releases with Dolby digital sound. Superb.

■ ■ UGC Cinemas
Mary Ann Street (029) 2066 7667
Located next to the new Springbok Bar and due to open later on this year, this cinema complex was still under construction at the time of going to print. Log onto the itchy website for info on the opening. All these end of review superlatives are incredibly witty. Magic.

■ ■ Theatres

■ ■ Chapter Arts Centre
Market Road, Canton (029) 2030 4400
Plays host to art exhibitions and installations, startling dance and theatre, poetry, obscure movies, and houses a restaurant and bar. Painfully pretentious clientele, but that's a small price to pay.

■ ■ New Theatre
Park Place (029) 2087 8889
Since 1906, the New has attracted some of the best names in theatre. Capturing the magic of Broadway in Cardiff with some impressive shows & musicals. Well worth a look, check the itchy website for more info.

Gr8 ENTERTAINMENT 4U

SLAP BANG IN THE MIDDLE OF CARDIFF

St David's Hall
Neuadd Dewi Sant
Cardiff 029 2087 8444

live music · top comedy · kids shows
& free art exhibitions

BOX OFFICE
029
2087
8889

big-name musicals · drama
dance & more

■ ■ Norwegian Church

Harbour Drive, Cardiff Bay (029) 2045 4899

A Norwegian café and arts centre which provides an esoteric range of entertainment from poetry to jazz. Its claim to fame is that Roald Dahl was baptised here in the days before Willy Wonka and Matilda had even entered his head.

Open daily 10-4pm, extended hours during the summer.

■ ■ Sherman Theatre

Senghennydd Road (029) 2064 6900

Commissions a vast range of plays and performances. A great place to catch new and first-time works. There's a lively ambience, enhanced by music in the foyer, making for one of the most sociable theatre evenings in town.

■ ■ St David's Hall

The Hayes (029) 2087 8444

To most people St David's Hall is known for its rather minging breeze block building, but it also hosts classical music, operas and proms. Not only this, but there's heaps of other stuff on offer such as live music and shows throughout the year from Stereophonics to Harry Hill. They also do their bit to keep the kids entertained with the 'Just Kidding' series. The likes of Rupert The Bear, The Chuckle Brothers and Mr Men have all made recent appearances and the hall also hosts the annual Disney awards. Performances aside there's a café, bar and restaurant all well worth a pre or post show visit. The hall also hosts the Welsh artist awards and displays during exhibits throughout the year. Check www.itchycardiff.co.uk for listings of music and stage events.

■ ■ Museums & Art Galleries

■ ■ National Museum and Gallery

Civic Centre, Cathay's Park (029) 2039 7951

Archaeology to Zoology are offered at Wales' biggest museum. Home to the world's largest leather back turtle and a hump backed whale – dead ones naturally, and lots of other 'look but don't touch' things from days of old. For those who insist on touching, try the Glanely gallery with its hands-on interactive exhibits, events and workshops. If art is your thing then you may be impressed to know that it houses the finest collection of impressionist paintings outside of France with works by Van Gogh, Monet and Cezanne. If art isn't your thing, you're reading the wrong section.

Opening times vary so ring in advance. Free admission.

■ ■ Museum of Welsh Life

St Fagans (029) 2057 3500

The mere mention of its name instills fear into the heart of every Welsh child. This a museum packed with parents trying desperately to convince the kids that history is fun. You'd think they'd remember from their own school days just how inspiring old stone cottages are. Anyway, this is one of Europe's biggest open-air museums. Visit and explore over 40 buildings which have been removed, transported and painstakingly rebuilt stone-by-stone. Watch real craftsmen at work as they imitate traditional skills and visit St Fagans castle complete with rose and organic gardens. It's the duty of every Welsh person to come along and see how their forefathers lived, but there's still plenty to interest those who don't stem from Cymru. You are never truly Welsh until you've been here.

Free admission.

Open Mon-Sun 10-5 (opening times may vary – ring to confirm).

■■ The Albany Gallery
Albany Road, Roath (029) 2048 7158

Don't be put off by the rather postcard looking images in their promotion as there's some genuinely interesting and contemporary work here. Providing you like that sort of thing obviously.

■■ Ffotogallery
**@ Chapter Arts Centre, Canton
(029) 2034 1667**

While it bids to establish the National Centre for Photography in Wales (anticipated to be in operation by autumn 2003) Ffotogallery will be temporarily based at Chapter. Expect the usual fascinating exhibitions and range of courses.

■■ G39
**39 Wyndham Arcade, Mill Lane
(029) 2025 5541**

Achingly contemporary installations regu-

larly changed. It's best to call, as the gallery i closed for a few days every month whils exhibitions change over.

■■ Howard Gardens Gallery
**Howard Gardens, UWIC Campus
(029) 2041 6638**

Full of art students swanning around bein all earnest about their work. It's free to ge in, so if you find yourself with nothing bette to do on an afternoon, you could do wors than try this place out.

■■ Llanover Hall Arts Centre
Romilly Road, Canton (029) 2063 1144

Even more out of the way than Chapte Provides lots of planned activity days an courses in the Arts. Also has digital facilitie and a photography darkroom. Get hold of current brochure.

■■ Martin Tinney Gallery
Windsor Place (029) 2064 1411

Somewhat tucked away, and somewha exclusive. Well worth checking out for con temporary work using traditional material (like paint). Just don't look at the prices i you suffer from vertigo.

Mon-Fri 10-6pm. Sat 10-5pm

■■ Activities

■■ Welsh International Climbing Centre
Bedlinog, South Wales (01443) 710 749

This may well be Wales' best kept secret fo

IT'S THE DREAM JOB.

hose of you who are into outdoor pursuits. uitable for all levels of climbers, with full quipment hire facilities, a sauna, and more mportantly, a decent bar area. The prices tart at £4 for students rising to £6.50, but re dependent on the time and day, so its best to phone ahead. Overnight stays are vailable in bunkhouses where prices start rom £8, and the centre's also due to open a ayaking centre and a dedicated caving and ot holing system.
Mon-Sun 10-10

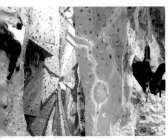

■■ Skate Extreme
Herbert Road, Newport (01633) 265 709
t helps to know what you're doing, but they welcome all forms of wheeled toys here provided you are willing to throw yourself down vert ramps and into the large oampit). There's 20,000 sq. ft. of purpose built course and prices start from £3.50 for n hour (non-members). Get on the blower to check prices. A top laugh.
Mon & Fri 12-8pm, Wed 12-9pm, Thurs 12-10, Sat & Sun 10-6, closed Tues.

■■■ Ski & Snowboard Centre
Fairwater Road, Fairwater (029) 2056 1793
Dry ski slope for snowboard and ski enthusiasts. Offers lessons by qualified instructors. Ring for more information.

■■■ Wales National Ice Rink
The Ice House, Hayes Bridge Road
(029) 2064 5988
Home of the Cardiff Devils and the only ice rink in South Wales. If you fancy a change or purely want to amuse yourself at the expense of others, skating definitely provides entertainment at little cost, and the added excitement of possible finger severage.

■■■ Task Force Paintball
Penllyn estate, Cowbridge (029) 2059 3900
Every so often we all wish we could gear up with some serious artillery and shoot our friends without fear of retribution. Well, Task Force lets you do so and offers a damn good day out in the process. Games can be arranged at any time for groups of 20 or more, and prices start at £25 for a half-day to £35 for a full day including lunch.

■■ Karting/Quad Bikes

■■ Llandow Karting
Llandow Circuit, Cowbridge
(01446) 795 568
A floodlit outdoor track. Arrive and drive or take part in grand prix events for groups or parties who feel the need for a bit of speed. £5-10 per hour. Mon-Sun 10.30-5.30

BUT YOU DON'T WANT TO LOOK DESPERATE.

■■■ Taff Valley Buggy Farm
Cwrt-y-Celyn farm, Upper Boat, Pontypridd
(029) 2083 1658

This place may be out in the sticks, but it's well worth the trip. Activities include quad biking around their cross country nature trail, archery, Land Rover driving and gorge walking. Open while the sun is shinin' and the weather is fine.

Fully inclusive cost of tour £14 or £16.50 per hr. Discounts for groups and students. Advance booking necessary.

Mon-Sun 9-8pm

■■■ Sports Grounds/Stadiums

■■■ Cardiff City Football Club
Ninian Park, Ninian Park Road
(029) 2022 1001

After promotion into the second division last season, the Bluebirds are flying high.

■■■ Cardiff Devils
The Ice House, Hayes Bridge
(029) 2064 5988

With more Canadians than you will find in Quebec the Devils are one of the top ice hockey teams in the country and send each visiting team home wishing them a sentence of eternal damnation.

■■■ Cardiff Rugby Club
The Arms Park, Westgate Street
(0870) 013 5213

The Arms Park stands in the shadow of the Millennium Stadium but that in no way

reflects on the rugby played here. With suc cesses in the league and in Europe in pas seasons, the Blue and Blacks present a daunting challenge to anyone who faces them.

■■■ Glamorgan Cricket Club
Sophia Gardens (029) 2040 9380

Despite struggling in the County Championship, they have a strong Sunday League side, and the squad is packed with young promising and handsome players "You were never interested before darling".

■■■ Days Out and Attractions

■■■ Cardiff Castle
Castle Street (029) 2087 8100

Every city should have one and we've got a big one, smack bang in the centre of the city The Romans built a bit, the Normans added a bit more and not to be out done, Lord Bute had to leave his mark on it as well. Pay a visit to the castle grounds and museums, then take a 50 minute tour of the interior. Top it off by eyeing up the beautiful Cardiffian

birds – the peacocks, obviously.
Mon-Sun Mar-Oct 9.30-6pm
Nov-Feb 9.30-4.30
Full tour Adults £5.25, Children & OAP's
£3.15, Students £4.20, Family £14.75
Grounds only Adults £2.60, Children & OAP's
£1.60, Students £2.10, Family £7.40

■ ■ Castell Coch
Tongwynlais, Cardiff (029) 2081 0101

A fairy-tale castle set on a hillside in wood-
land overlooking a gorge in the Taff valley.
Built on the site of the 13th century Castell
Coch (the Red Castle) by Lord Bute to
emphasise the fact that he was reputedly
the richest man in the world at the time.
With a working portcullis and drawbridge,
Castell Coch is a feast of decoration, detail
and illusion.
Open end Mar-end May 9.30-5pm, end May-
end Sept 9.30-6pm, Oct-end Mar 9.30-4pm
Mon-Sat (11-4pm Sun)
Adults £2.50, conc. £2.00, Family £7 Children
under 5 free

■ ■ The Millennium Stadium – Tours
Stadium Shop, Gate 3, Westgate Street (029) 2082 2228

The home of Welsh rugby presents The
Millennium Stadium, formerly known as the
formidable Arms Park. Nations would trem-
ble here in days gone by, but the marvel of a
nation's pride and an engineering achievement makes this the envy of the world. Now
you can capture the magic, passion and
electric atmosphere that sets Welsh rugby
apart from the rest by visiting the stadium
as part of a tour.
Mon-Sat 10-6, Sun 10-5
Adult £5, Children (5-16) £2.50, OAP's,
Students, unemployed £3, family ticket £15

■ ■ Techniquest
Stuart Street, Cardiff Bay (029) 2047 5475

A fun-filled, hands-on science exhibition,
guaranteed to amuse and entertain adults
and children alike. Try the musiquest, sci-
ence theatre or for an extra 75p take a voy-
age of discovery into outer space in the
planetarium (booking advised).
Just as your brain kicks into overload take a
rest in the waterfront café. Phone or log onto
the itchy site to get details of special events.
Mon-Fri 9.30-4.30pm, school hols 9.30-5pm,
Sat,Sun & bank hols 10.30-5pm
Last admission 45 min B4 closing
Adult £6, Children (5-16) & concessions £4,
Family ticket (2adults & 3 children) £16.50
Planetarium 75p extra
Discovery Room 50p extra

■■■ Big Pit Mining Museum

Blaenavon (01495) 790311

You'll need a motor to get there, but it's worth it for a novel day out. It's just like the real thing apparently – they'll dress you as a miner, take you down the mines, tell you tales of tragedy, get you working 'til your family depend on the income, and then sack you with no alternative employment.

Mar-Nov 9.30-5pm 7 days a week, underground tours run frequently from 10-3.30, phone for winter opening times.

Free Admission

■■■ Parks

Cardiff has a wide variety of parks to admire and enjoy. Bute park, which is behind the castle, houses an arboretum and joins up with Sophia gardens which is part of the Taff trail. Heath Park and Roath Park are the largest on the Roath side of the city. The main feature of Roath park is the boating lake. Pedloes and rowing boats are available for hire, whist Heath Park houses a small golf course. Victoria Park off the Cowbridge Road, Llandaff Fields at the top of Cathedral Road and Thompson Park in Canton are popular retreats for those trying to forget that they live in a bustling city.

■■■ Cosmeston Lakes

Lavernock Road, Penarth (029) 2070 1678

This park consists of over 90 hectares of countryside and woodlands. Lakes and wetlands dominate the landscape and a reconstructed 14th century medieval village is built on the original site. Laugh at the out-of-work actors as fully clothed, remarkably preserved villagers, who will take you on a tour of the village. Explore the museum and visitor centre and take note of the special events held throughout the year.

Visitor Centre open Summer 10-6 (village 11-5). Winter 10-5 (village 11-4)

Free parking and entry to the park. Medieval Village Adult £3, Children & OAP's £2, Family £6.50

■■■ Dyfryn Gardens

St Nicholas, Cardiff (029) 2059 3328

This Grade 1 Edwardian garden (currently being restored to its full glory) will continually stun you with its variety of colour and form all year round. Special events are organised throughout the year.

Open 10 'til early evening

Apr – end Oct, Adults £3, Children & OAP's £2, family £6.50. Free at all other times.

■■■ Strip Clubs

■■■ The Fantasy Lounge

93 St Mary Street (029) 2038 2201/2

See club review and listings for more.

■■■ Bowling

■■■ Megabowl

376 Newport Road (029) 2046 1666

Take your pick of the 26 bowling alleys

which is just as well because there isn't much choice when it comes to selecting your shoes. If you don't want to follow the 'silly shoe' fashion then the dodgems and arcade games may be more up your street.
Mon-Fri 12pm-11pm, Sat & Sun 10am-11.30pm
1 Game Adult £4.75, Child £4.25 but look out for regular offers.

■■ Hollywood Bowl
Atlantic Wharf Leisure Village, Cardiff Bay (029) 2047 1444
Numerous alleys to aim your balls, I mean bowls. If you're not interested in shuffling your balls there are video games, pool and Bar Original for a drink and a snack.
Mon-Fri 12-12, Sat & Sun 10-12
1 Game. Adult £2.50, Children £1.75 12-6pm Mon-Fri or £3.75 and £2.75 6pm-close, weekends and bank holidays.

■■ Snooker/Pool

■■ Rileys Pool & Snooker Club
Wellington Street, Canton (029) 2039 0322
Open 24 hours

■■ Rileys Snooker Club
52-54 City Road Roath (029) 2049 3694

■■ Rajahs Pool Club
62-64 Lower Cathedral Road (029) 2039 5460
Mon-Sun 7-12am

■■ Internet Cafes

■■ The Cardiff Cyber Café Ltd
9 Duke Street (1st Floor) (029) 2023 5757
Independent café offering fast internet access as well as scanning, faxing, printing, CD writing, courses, web design, hosting and more.
Mon-Fri 10-7pm, Sat 10-6pm, Sun 11-5pm

■■ Cardiff Internet Café
15-17 Wyndham Arcade (029) 2023 2313
Mon-Sat 9.30-9pm, Sun 10-7pm

■■ Internet Exchange
8 Church Street (029) 2023 6047
Mon-Sat 9-9pm, Sun 10-7pm

■■ Urban Retreat
104 Crwys Road, Roath (029) 2040 3420
Mon-Fri 10am-8pm, Sat & Sun 10-4

■■ Live Music Venues

■■ Cardiff International Arena
Mary Ann Street
General Enquiries (029) 2023 4500
Booking (029) 2022 4488
Cardiff's biggest and best music venue. It

www.reddragonfm.co.uk RED DRAGON 103.2•97.4 FM

...EVERYONE WELCOME

TENPIN BOWLING
LICENCED BARS
WIMPY DINERS
AMERICAN POOL
AMUSEMENT AREAS
QUASAR
AND SO MUCH MORE*

TO FIND YOUR NEAREST MEGABOWL VISIT OUR WEBSI
OR CALL TALKING PAGES FREE ON 0800 600 900

*Facilities vary at each Megabowl

www.megabowl.co.uk

will set your eardrums ringing with the sounds of pop, rock, R&B and indie to name just a few. Also hosts exhibitions and conferences.

■ ■ The Coal Exchange
Cardiff Bay (029) 2049 4917

A beautiful building steeped in history hosting rock, pop and classical concerts and not a piece of coal in sight.
Office open Mon-Fri 9-5pm

■ ■ Wales National Ice Rink
The Ice House, Hayes Bridge Road (029) 2064 5988

Call for listings info.

■ ■ St David's Hall
The Hayes (029) 2087 8444

Has entertained world famous orchestras, tribute bands and singers but has diversified into many other areas of music and entertainment. The likes of Ocean Colour Scene and Harry Hill have appeared here.

■ ■ Millennium Stadium
Westgate Street (029) 2082 2228

With its sliding roof this is the biggest undercover arena in Europe so it's only fitting that it should attract the biggest of the big in pop and rock icons. Tina Turner has played here and 2001 has seen the likes of Robbie

Williams, Bon Jovi and the Stereophonics – not that I'm name dropping.

■ ■ Cardiff Castle
Castle Street (029) 2087 8100

Hosts open air concerts inside the castle grounds. Red Dragon's 'Party in the Park' has become an annual fixture and the likes of Bryan Adams, Sting and our very own Tom Jones and the Stereophonics have competed with the cries of the resident peacocks who are fast becoming regular little rock chicks.

■ ■ Casinos

■ ■ Grosvenor Casino
Greyfriars Road (029) 2034 2991

■ ■ Les Croupier
32 St Mary Street (029) 2038 2810

■ ■ Comedy

■ ■ The Glee Comedy Club
Mermaid Quay, Cardiff Bay 0870 241 5093

Cardiff has missed out on the comedy circuit for years but those dark days are behind us. The Glee Club is a recent addition to the bay, plunging it into the world of humour and light hearted fun, and has much to offer in the way of those well known faces as well as the up and coming stand up comedians. When the laughter is brought under control the disco gets under way. Alternatively try Ceroc French style dancing on a Monday night. Top venue.
Doors open 8pm (7.45 Sat) Show 9pm – booking advised.
Fri £10.50, (£5 NUS) followed by disco, Sat £12.50 (£10 NUS) followed by disco.

www.itchycardiff.co.uk

■ ■ ■ Chameleon Beauty Clinic
14c Whitchurch Road (029) 2052 1251
Fortunately you won't come out looking like
Boy George even if you do get the urge to
sing like him.
Tue 8-7, Wed 9.30-7 Thu & Fri 9.30-6, Sat 8-2
Revitalising facial treatment - 30 mins £15

■ ■ ■ Creative Nails & Beauty
10 Charles Street (029) 2066 6405
Offers everything to do with nails.
Mon-Sat 9-6
Basic manicure £10

■ ■ ■ The Nail Centre
Capital Arcade (029) 2066 5995
The complete nail service from manicures to
nail jewellery.
Mon-Sat 9-5.30
French Manicure £19.95

■ ■ ■ Harlington Skin & Beauty Clinic
14 Churchill Way (029) 2022 7049
Pamper yourself like a pedigree poodle but
remember this place is not for dogs, it's for
refined females.
Mon-Thu 9-7 Fri-Sat 9-5.30
Acupuncture without needles 20 mins £20

■ ■ ■ Tan 'N Go
52 Charles Street (029) 2022 5654
Cardiff's premier vertical sunbed centre and
voted the best performing units by the
Sunbed Association. Walk on in, three minutes later, walk out. Literally tan 'n' go. If only
everything in life was this simple, we'd be
able to smoke gear all day long.
Tues-Sat 9.30-5.30
VT 2000 upright fast sun shower - 3 min £4

■ ■ Hairdressing

■ ■ Mens

■ ■ The Barber Shop
35 Cathedral Road, Poncanna
(029) 2038 4838
Mon-Fri 9-5.45, Sat 9-4.45
Dry Cut £8.50

■ ■ Bentley & Co
Andrews Arcade, Queen Street
(029) 2066 4911

Barbers that offers a 'total grooming concept'. The shop is furnished with a bar, a wide range of reading material and cable television. They specialise in all kinds of haircuts, traditional lather shaves, facial massages as well as advice on common skin irritations (this doesn't mean how to get rid of the wife). Mon-Wed, Fri 9-6, Sat 9-5, late opening Thu 'til 8
Wet Cut from £9

■ ■ City Barbers
2 Charles Street (029) 2022 2530
Mon-Fri 8-6, Sat 9-5
Wet cut & blow-dry £9.50

■ ■ Stanmate & Stunell Barbers
84 City Road (029) 2063 1050
Sounds like a toilet make, but it's actually a very good salon.
Mon-Fri 9.30-5.30, Sat 9-4
Wash and cut £12.50

■ ■ Unisex

■ ■ Bauhaus Hair Shop
Unit 1 Dominions Arcade
(029) 2023 3005
Mon-Fri 9-6, Sat 9-5
Men £27, Women £30

■ ■ Coray & Co
126 City Road, Roath (029) 2048 1481
A real 'top-to-toe' service and a prestigious salon. Learn the finer points of body groom-

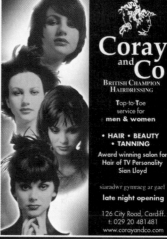

ing, tanning and hair trends, all under the same roof. Excellent all round and great value.
Mon-Wed, Fri, Sat 9-6, late opening Thu 'til 8
Men £16.90, Women £26.90

■ ■ ■ Essentials Hairdressing
1st & 2nd floors, 8 St John Square (029) 2037 4448
Mugs and mullets all trimmed here.
Mon-Fri 9-6, Sat 9-5
Men £20, Women £27

■ ■ ■ Gavin Alexander
14 Queen's Arcade (029) 2064 5555
'Fresh start, pure style, right here, right now' is their motto and that's what you get. Stylists who are genuinely interested in your hair and not your next holiday to Benidorm, oh no. Wicked designer salon that rates high in the itchy style guide.
Mon-Wed, Fri 9.30-6, Sat 9-5, late opening Thu 'til 8
Men £16, Women £26

■ ■ ■ Ken Picton Hair and Spa
Mermaid Quay, Cardiff Bay (029) 2066 2080
Trendy, innovative and one of Cardiff's biggest success stories. Swanky salon.
Mon-Wed, Fri, Sat 9-6, late opening Thu 'til 8
Men £18, Women £25

■ ■ ■ Lazarou Brothers
12 Churchill Way (029) 2038 7220
Mon-Wed 10-6, Thurs, Fri 10-7, Sat 9-5
Men £8, Women £20

■ ■ ■ Saks Hair & Beauty
11 St John Street (029) 2038 2525
The UK's leading salon group renowned fo pampering at its best - a visit promises to be a treat with a difference.
Mon, Wed 10-6, Tue 10-8, Thu 9-8, Fri 9-7, Sa 9-6, Sun 11-6
Men £20, Women £30

■ ■ ■ Toni & Guy
35 St Mary Street (029) 2039 9900
Mon-Wed, Fri 9-6, Sat 9-5, late opening Thurs 'til 7
Men £23, Women £30

■ ■ ■ Tattoos and Piercing

■ ■ ■ Rebel/Rebel and Skin Thre
31-33 Wyndham Arcade (029) 2064 5069
Piercings from £4
Mon-Sat 9.30-4pm

■ ■ ■ Rave
Cowbridge Road East (029) 2056 6950
Tooth Jewel £10
Mon-Sat 11-5.30, closed Wed

gavin alexander
hairdressing

opening times
mon-wed 9.30-6
thurs 9.30-8
fri 9.30-6
sat 9-5

**14 Queens Arcade
Cardiff CF10 2BY
t: 02920 645555**

www.gavinalexander.co.uk
Student discount available

Dalry, 51, Painter/decorator

So, after a hard day's slog on walls where do you hit the tiles?
RSVP – the one that used to be Owains

And for clubbing?
I don't. Too boring, sorry

I didn't want to be ageist. How about for a meal then?
Cutting Edge is reliably good

Best thing about Cardiff?
Police with attitude

And the worst?
Middle age

■ ■ ■ Blue Banana
23 Caroline Street (029) 2022 3911
Prices from £10
Mon-Sat 9.30-4.30pm

■ ■ ■ Skin Creation Tattoo Studio
132 Broadway, Roath (029) 2049 4804
Small Dragon from £25
Mon-Sat 11-4.30pm

■ ■ ■ Doc Grahams Tattoo Land
87 Tudor Street (029) 2022 6286
Celtic Band from £25

■ ■ ■ Leisure Centres

■ ■ ■ Western Leisure Centre
Caerau Lane (029) 2059 3592
Pool, gym, fitness studio with a range of classes, bar and creche facilities.
Mon-Sat 7.30-10.30pm, Sun 9-5.30pm

■ ■ ■ Maindy Leisure Centre
Crown Way (029) 2052 9230
Pool, gym and bar.
Mon-Wed 6.30-10.15pm, Thu 6.30-4.30, Sat 8
Sun 7.30-5.30pm

■ ■ ■ Eastern Leisure Centre
Llanrumney Avenue (029) 2079 6616
Pool, gym, bar and creche facilities.
Mon-Sat 7.30-11pm, Sun 8.30-6pm

■ ■ ■ Llanishen Leisure Centre
Ty Glas Avenue (029) 2076 2411
Pool with slide, gym and fitness studio offering a variety of fitness classes, tanning facilities and bar.
Mon-Fri 7.30-9pm, Sat 10-5.30, Sun 9-8pm

■ ■ ■ Welsh Institute of Sport
Sophia Gardens (off Cathedral Road) (029) 2030 0500
This is the best of the best when it comes to sports. Situated next to Glamorgan cricket club. Sports halls contain netball, basketball and badminton courts as well as individu

quash courts, all with spectator viewing. Outside you'll find floodlit astro-turf pitch sed for hockey and football. The institute osts many international events in hockey, etball, squash etc. A well kitted out weights oom is used by athletes and all those serius about keeping fit. Facilities also include wimming pool and sauna.
Mon-Fri 8-9.30pm, Sat & Sun 8.15-9.30pm

■ ■ Health Clubs

■ ■ Cannons
Welsh National Tennis Centre, Ocean Park, Cardiff Bay (029) 2045 6000
Put your body through its paces in the fitness studio and gym, sweat it out in the team room and sauna, pamper it in the pool then relax in the café and members bar. With added features of adventure activity trips and external events. Creche facilities for the little nippers for when they get under our feet – must be collected on departure.
Monthly Membership £35-£43
Mon-Fri 7-11pm, Sat 8-11pm, Sun 8-11pm

■ ■ Body Matters
Unit 1+2 Wesley Hall, Bridge Street (029) 2066 8600
Complete gym facility in the centre of town. Gym, free weights, tanning beds and sauna.
Monthly Membership £28
Sun 10am-2pm, Mon-Thurs 7am-9pm, Fri 7am-8pm, Sat 10am-4pm

■ ■ Fitness First
Rover Way, Pengam (029) 2049 5115
Cowbridge Road West (029) 2059 8899
Two branches recently opened in the city providing all leisure facilities and a creche.
Monthly Membership £23-£33
Sun 8-10pm, Mon-Fri 6.30-10pm, Sat 8-9pm

■ ■ Lady in Leisure
1-2 Castle Street (029) 2034 4331
Full of career girls on lunch break or bored housewives filling their time by burning those calories in the gym and sauna.
Sun 10-5, Mon-Thurs 9-9, Fri 11-9, Sat 10-5pm

■ ■ Peak Physique
Rhymney River Bridge (029) 2046 2040
Weights gym with serious clientele, no joggers in sight here. Monthly membership £28
Sun 9-2, Mon-Fri 9-9, Sat 9-6

www.reddragonfm.co.uk RED DRAGON 103.2·97.4 FM

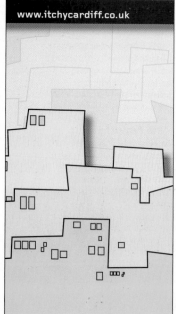
www.itchycardiff.co.uk

Pizza & Burgers

Dominos Pizza
62 Crwys Road (029) 2022 9977
200 Cowbridge Road (029) 2023 2000
Delivery. Open 'til 1am Sat.

Piero's
185 Cowbridge Road (029) 2022 7060
The real McCoy when it comes to Italian food. Choose from a selection of pasta, pizza and antipasti. Free garlic bread with every pizza or pasta takeaway. Open 'til 11pm.

Burger King
12-14 Queen Street (029) 2034 1555
473 Newport Road (029) 2045 6057
Open 'til 12 in the week, 3am Fri/Sat

McDonald's
Queen Street (029) 2022 2604
St Mary Street (029) 2034 5986
Newport Road (029) 2045 1050
St Mary Street open 'til 3am w/end

Chicken

Chicken Cottage
St Mary Street (029) 2034 4598
/ 2034 4597
Where Miss Millie lives. Probably.
Open 'til 1am in the week, 3am Sat.

Kentucky Fried Chicken
Queen Street (029) 2039 4270
Open 'til 12am

Miss Millies
231 Cowbridge Road (029) 2039 6116
Open 'til 1am in the week, 4am weekends

▪▪ Fish & Chips

▪▪ Albany Road Fish Bar
8 Albany Road (029) 2048 2022
Open 'til 12am

▪▪ Devonia
79 Whitchurch Road (029) 2061 9478
Open 'til 12am

▪▪ Dorothys
39/40 Caroline Street (029) 2064 5813
Open 'til 4am Sat

▪▪ Harry Ramsdens
Stuart Street, Cardiff Bay
(029) 2046 3334
Open 'til 10.30/11 in the week, 9.30pm Sun

▪▪ Indian

▪▪ The Balti Empire
157-159 Albany Road (029) 2048 5757
The Empire strikes back with their own balti.
Delivery. Open 'til 11.45pm

▪▪ Balti Wallah
2 Cowbridge Road (029) 2023 1227
Delivery. Open 'til 12.30

▪▪ Juboraj
Lake Road West, Roath (029) 2045 5123
1 Heol y Deri, Rhiwbina (029) 2062 8894
0 Mill Lane, Town Centre (029) 2037 7669

▪▪ Chinese

▪▪ The China Kitchen
Albany Road (029) 2049 5488
Open 'til 12am

▪▪ Happy Gathering
233 Cowbridge Road (029) 2039 7531
A stunning restaurant which does takeaway on request. Open 'til 8pm.

▪▪ Noble House Peking Cuisine
133 Albany Road, Roath (029) 2049 3490 / 2047 2929
Open 'til 11pm

▪▪ Sandwiches / Pastry

▪▪ Cornish Bakehouse
11 Church Street (029) 2066 5041
Open 'til 6pm

▪▪ Cornish Pasty Bake Away
34 High Street (029) 2039 0815
Open 'til 6pm

▪▪ Daiquiris
Salisbury Road (029) 2034 4807
Open 'til 11pm

▪▪ Dough
20 Salisbury Road (029) 2022 2888
Open 'til 4pm

▪▪ La Baguette
105 Queen Street (029) 2022 0227
Open 'til 4.30pm

▪▪ Nibblets
200 Whitchurch Road (029) 2052 2084
Doesn't sound very filling but has the best takeaway salads in town. Open 'til 2.30pm

▪▪ That Baguette Place
32 Royal Arcade (029) 2022 3158
Open 'til 5.30pm

useful info

www.itchycardiff.co.uk

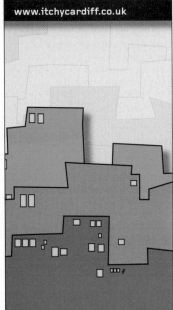

■■ Travel

Getting about in Cardiff is relatively easy if you have a car, but there's plenty of buses, trains and taxis roaming around. Alternatively you could look a complete tool and use a micro scooter.

■■ Taxis

Capital Cars Ltd ....(029) 2077 7777
Premier ....(029) 2055 5555
Black Cabs ....(029) 2034 3343
Central Taxis ....(029) 2066 6333

■■ Buses

Cardiff Bus 0870 608 2608
Central Station ....(029) 2039 6521
National Express 0870 5808080

■■ Trains

Valley Lines..............................08457 484950
National Rail Enquiries..........08457 484950
Wales and West Rail 0870 9000 777

■■ Airport

Cardiff Wales Airport ....(01446) 711 111

■ ■ Tourist Information

Cardiff Visitors Centre........(029) 2022 7281
Cardiff Bay Visitor Centre (029) 2046 3833

■ ■ Car Hire

Avis
14-22 Tudor Street.................(029) 2034 2111
24 hour reservations 0870 60 60 100

Charter Vehicle Hire
25 Station Road, Llandaff North
....(029) 2055 3111/1251

Enterprise Rent-A-Car
5 Penarth Road......................(029) 2038 9222

Hertz
Central Square, City Centre
....(029) 2022 4548/9

■ ■ Van Hire (also car rentals)

Charter Vehicle Hire
25 Station Road, Llandaff North
....(029) 2055 3111/1251

Thrifty
Bessemer Road ....(029) 2038 7777

■ ■ Other

Cardiff Cats & Water Buses (029) 2048 8842
Shopmobility – Cardiff ......(029) 2039 9355

■ ■ Media

In the unlikely event that we've missed out any vital information – this list of local media may come in handy.

■ ■ Entertainment & Listings

itchy Cardiff – The insider's guide for all things entertainment. Available at Waterstone's, WH Smith, Virgin, HMV, but to keep up with what's going on day-to-day, log onto **www.itchycardiff.co.uk**, or if you can't be bothered rummaging around for the info you want, sign up for our SMS text messages and let it come to you.

Buzz – A well respected, free monthly magazine covering the latest news, dance promos and information on all of the entertainment highs and lows in Cardiff. Copies can be found at several points throughout the city centre but you've gotta be quick as copies go like ear muffs in Siberia.

City Nights – They call it Cardiff's hottest guide but we somehow beg to differ. Scarcely seen or available, but then it is free so you can't moan too much.

www.reddragonfm.co.uk RED DRAGON 103.2•97.4 FM

Cardiff Visitors Guide – Produced by the Welsh Tourist Board and available to buy at gift shops and the tourist info centres. Comprehensive and compact.

Welsh Bands Weekly – The title says it all, just be careful which side you read as it's bilingual. If you don't come from Wales it'll look like a load of gibberish. Available from Virgin stores for a few quid. We like it.

R U Sorted – Freebie mag that profiles dance promoters, club nights, bands and DJs. Credible and informative. Available in the city centre and surrounding areas.

The Fly – Quality freebie magazine. Available from Bar Fly. Features bands and profiles artists. Provides highly informative reading for all rockers out there.

NRG Lifestyle – Does what it says on the front. All about your lifestyle from sport to body. For the young professional and distributed free.

Elite – Full of fashion, interiors and beauty tips, modelling itself on Vogue-type periodicals. Ideal monthly mag for professional 30-something women.

Ladies First – 'The first choice magazine for women in South, East and West Wales'. Be that their dream or a reality it certainly keeps you up-to-date with all of the dirt and gossip as well as the usual fashion and beauty that you might expect.

■ ■ Local Newspapers

South Wales Echo – Local paper covering local and national stories as they break. Makes for thrilling reading if you enjoy following current events such as the lady from Blaenavon who lost her tabby cat and the follow up of how they were reunited. Distributed at all newsagents, corner shops and on every street corner – just listen out as the indistinguishable bellows and moans of 'echo' fill the air.

Western Mail – More comprehensive newspaper covering the bigger stories in Wales. Good arts and current affairs coverage.

■ ■ Student Media

Gair Rhydd – Student newspaper with a less than traditional approach.

■ ■ Radio

Red Dragon FM 103.2, 97.4 FM – A highly popular commercial radio station in the South. It appeals to all ages playing mainly commercial chart/cheese, R&B and dance.

Real Radio 105.7 – New addition to Cardiff attracting a slightly older listeners. Plays chart, golden oldies and other granny music.

Galaxy 101 – Cardiff and Bristol's answer to the clubbing and dance scene with respected DJs and cracking line-ups.

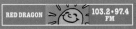

RED DRAGON 103.2 · 97.4 FM **www.reddragonfm.co.uk**

There's better things to spend money on.
Don't waste it on travel.

If you're under 26 or a student save £££'s on travel with a Young Persons' Discount Coachcard. Cards cost £9 and save you up to 30% off already low fares all year. Register online to receive special offers throughout the year.

For journey planning, tickets and coachcards

visit GoByCoach.com or call 08705 80 80 80

Check online for details.
Coach services depart from Bus Station, Cardiff.

accommodation

www.itchycardiff.co.uk

Prices are per person, per night, including breakfast and are based on two sharing.

■■ Expensive

■■ Angel Hotel
Castle Street (029) 2064 9200
£65 Week £39 W/end

■■ Hilton
Kingsway (029) 2064 6300
Five star hotel in the centre of Cardiff.
£62.50 Week £62.50 W/end

■■ The International Hotel
**Schooner Way, Atlantic Wharf
(029) 2047 5000**
£60 Week £60 W/end

■■ Jury's Hotel
Mary Ann Street (029) 2034 1441
£73 Week £35 W/end

■■ Marriot
Mill Lane (029) 2039 9944
£65.50 Week £44 W/end

■ ■ St David's Hotel
Havannah Street, Cardiff Bay
(029) 2045 4045
The first five star hotel complex to come to
Cardiff. An architectural feat that can be
seen everywhere in the bay.
£98.50 Week £65 W/end

■ ■ Thistle Hotel
Park Place (029) 2038 3471
£75 Week £46 W/end

■ ■ Mid Priced

■ ■ Cardiff Moat House
Circle Way East, Llanederyn
(029) 2058 9988
£55 Week £49 W/end

■ ■ Churchills
Cardiff Road, Llandaff (029) 2040 1300
£45 Week £45 W/end

■ ■ Express by Holiday Inn
Schooner Way, Atlantic Wharf
(029) 2044 9000
£31 Week £25 W/end

■ ■ The Post House Cardiff City
Castle Street 0870 400 8140
£57 Week £44.45 W/end

■ ■ Sandringhan Hotel
St Mary Street (029) 2023 2161
£60 Week £60 W/end

■ ■ Budget

■ ■ Big Sleep Hotel
Bute Terrace (029) 2063 6363
£29 Week £22.50 W/end

■ ■ Cardiff Backpacker
98 Neville Street, Riverside
(029) 2034 5577
Dormitory £14
Private Single £21
Private Double £33

■ ■ Courtlands Hotel
110 Newport Road (029) 2049 7583
£25 Week £25 W/end

■ ■ Riverbank Hotel
53-59 Despenser Street, Riverside
(029) 2037 8866
£25 Week £21 W/end

■ ■ Academic Accommodation

(Seasonal availability)

■ ■ (UWCC)
Conference Officer
Southgate House
Bevan Place
(029) 2087 4027

■ ■ University of Wales Institute, Cardiff
Cyncoed Campus, Cyncoed Road
(029) 2041 6182

It's YOUR Red Dragon FM

ALL DAY EVERY DAY

index

	Grid Ref.	Pg. no

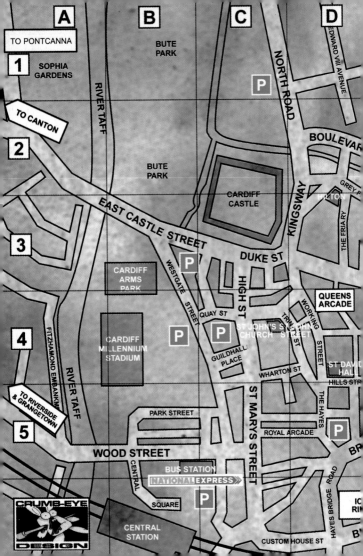

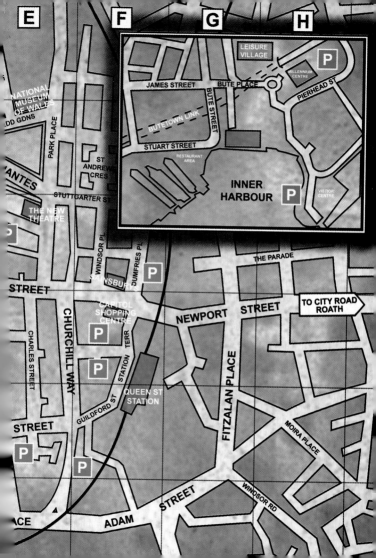